日本百味
散步帳

THE WONDERFUL & DELICIOUS IN JAPAN

凱琳・芙爾斯
KAILENE FALLS

涂紋凰 譯

前言

2018年我畫了第一幅水彩食物插圖，那是一串便利商店的三色糯米丸。因為實在太好玩，所以才想繼續畫各種日本的美食。抱著輕鬆的心情開始的小興趣，讓我逐漸了解日本飲食文化的美好與美味，不知不覺間，光是食物的畫作就超過數百幅。

本書不只是匯集食物插畫的藝術書籍，同時也匯集身為美國人的我，來到日本之後，對日本飲食文化與歷史的所思所想。但願各位在閱讀時，這些資訊能夠為您帶來樂趣，並且幫助各位發現，日本美好與美味的事物。

PREFACE

My first watercolor food illustration was this convenience store dango that I painted in 2018. I enjoyed the process so much that I decided to try painting various other foods I found in Japan. While this started as a casual hobby, I gradually began to discover the wonderful and delicious depths of Japanese food culture. Before I realized it, I had painted hundreds of Japanese foods.

This book is not just a food illustration art book. It is also a collection of realizations and thoughts of an American in Japan regarding the culture and history of Japanese food. I hope that those reading this will find the information interesting and will use it as a guide to learning about "The Wonderful & Delicious in Japan."

CONTENTS

提 醒

· 本書刊載資訊為 2022 年 3～5 月內容。
· 原則上，刊載金額為含稅價。
· 掃描「SHOP INFO」的 QR Code 會顯示 Google 地圖上的店家位置。
· 為了讓讀者能夠容易理解，中文和英文的內容有些許差異。
· 本書出版後，內容與金額有可能會改變，造訪之前請再次確認。

DISCLAIMER

· The contents reflect information current between March and May, 2022.
· The prices listed include sales tax.
· The QR Codes on the SHOP INFO pages indicate the Google Map locations.
· The Mandarin and English information differs in some sections in order to
  make the contents more easily understood by the readers.
· Prices and information may have changed since publication.
  Please be aware of this before visiting these locations.

4 5 6
月 月 月

SPRING

April
May
June

春天是我最喜歡的季節。隨著氣溫漸暖，百花依次盛開，
可以欣賞梅花、紫藤、櫻花等各種花朵。
而且，此時也是許多美味甜點登場的季節喔！

Spring is my favorite season. The warmer weather brings
blooming flowers and visits to gardens
filled with wisteria, plum, and cherry blossoms.
Many gorgeous desserts take the stage this time of year too!

櫻花甜點

櫻花季節不只能賞櫻，還可以吃到櫻花甜點！
在歐美，能品嚐到鮮花味道的甜點非常稀奇，
但是日本的櫻花甜點已有數百年的歷史。
現在2～4月會推出很多期間限定的和菓子和洋菓子，
成為春季的一大享受。

Sakura aren't just pretty to look at; they also make beautiful desserts. While flower-flavored desserts are unusual in the West, Japan has hundreds of years of history creating desserts based on cherry blossoms. From February to April, you can find sakura desserts of both Japanese and Western traditions, another reason to look forward to springtime.

APR.
4月的回憶

——————— at ———————

飛鳥山公園
Asukayama Park

賞櫻的景點很多，所以我喜歡每年去不同地方賞櫻。截至目前為止最讓我感動的景點，是距離新宿車站搭電車30分鐘左右的飛鳥山公園。那裡空間寬廣，可以花幾個小時散步、享受櫻花美景。

There are many sakura-viewing spots, and every year I try to hit a different one. About 30 minutes from Shinjuku is one of my favorite sakura locations, Asukayama Park. It's absolutely massive, and you can easily spend hours walking and enjoying the views.

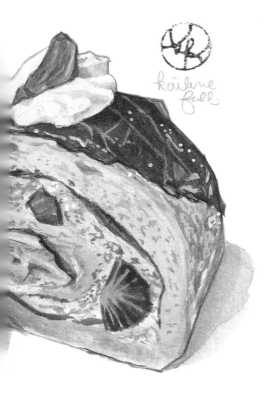

01 櫻花蛋糕
Sakura Cake

蒙布朗SAKURA & SAKURA蛋糕捲

KIHACHI甜點專賣店 東大島
648日圓／627日圓

有很多甜點使用櫻花和花瓣裝飾，但「櫻花味」通常不是來自櫻花，而是鹽漬櫻花葉產生的風味。這種花香來自櫻花葉中的「香豆素」。用鹽漬過的櫻花葉和櫻花，搭配草莓、樹莓、紅豆沙等配料，這是一款加入日本風味的西洋甜點。

※插畫呈現的商品為春季限定款。

Mont Blanc SAKURA & SAKURA Roll

PATISSERIE KIHACHI
Higashi-Ojima Store
¥648 / ¥627

While many sakura sweets use flowers and petals for decoration, the classic "sakura flavor" doesn't come from the flower. Instead, it comes from a chemical called coumarin which is found in the leaves and provides the distinct floral "cherry blossom flavor." For these cakes, sakura leaves were combined with flavors such as strawberry, raspberry, and bean paste to make unique fusion desserts.

※This illustration features a product only available in spring.

櫻花炸彈

Cinnabon・西雅圖貝斯特咖啡
六本木店
346日圓

我在美國的時候就很喜歡肉桂捲專賣店「Cinnabon」，一聽到有提供純季節限定的櫻花口味，就心想「一定要畫這個」。肉桂捲淋上杏仁與櫻花風味的糖霜，兩者搭配絕妙，粉色的脆片在畫面上也很有張力。雖然很甜，但是配咖啡一起吃就剛剛好！

※ 販售時間為 2021 年 2 月～3 月（目前沒有販售）。

Sakurabon

Cinnabon • Seattle's Best Coffee
Roppongi Store
¥346

I've loved Cinnabon since I was in America, and when I saw that Cinnabon Japan was making a limited-time sakura-flavored bun, I knew I had to paint it. The balance of the cinnamon roll with the almond and cherry-blossom-flavored frosting was fantastic. The crumble on top added an extra pop of texture, perfect for illustrating. Yes, it was sweet. But alongside a cup of coffee, it was just perfect!

※This product was available February to March, 2021(Not currently for sale).

02 SHOP INFO → P040

03 抹茶與櫻花和菓子
Matcha and Sakura Wagashi

3種和菓子套餐＆宇治抹茶
簡單的夢想 日本橋別邸
1300日圓／700日圓

我個人覺得很多櫻花和菓子的櫻花味都太
重，因此找到「簡單的夢想」這家和菓子
酒吧的時候，我非常感動。這裡除了傳統
的和菓子之外，也有能搭配酒或茶一起吃
的特殊和菓子。譬如櫻花羊羹搭配零陵香
豆，還有白豆沙搭配起司蛋糕！是一間擅
長搭配意外食材的現代和菓子店。

Triple Wagashi Set & Uji Matcha
kantan na yume Nihonbashi Store
¥1300 / ¥700

I find many traditional sakura sweets to be a
bit too intense in flavor, so I was pleasantly
surprised to find "Kantan na Yume," an unusual
bar that serves alcohol and tea along with
wagashi (Japanese sweets). The owner makes
classic wagashi but also experiments by
combining traditional desserts such as sakura
yokan and nerikiri with unique flavors like tonka
beans and cheesecake. A delicious modern take
on classic Japanese sakura sweets!

水果聖代

在美國能吃到的水果聖代非常樸素，
就是優格加入水果與燕麥片的早餐。
聖代原本誕生於法國，
但是日本的聖代是從美國傳入，
後來獨自進化成非常豪華的甜點。

Parfaits eaten in America are simple: usually a breakfast item made of yogurt, fruit, and granola. While originating in France, the Japanese parfait is inspired by the American dessert, just taken to a whole new and luxurious level.

FRUIT PARFAITS

三莓聖代
果實園里貝爾
2400日圓

說到聖代，經典的配料就是「草莓」對吧。因為很想畫草莓聖代，所以找到果實園里貝爾的聖代時，我就想著「一定要畫下來」。配料的草莓不只露出外側，還精心用漂亮的剖面堆疊，加上藍莓與麝香葡萄做跳色搭配，以插畫家的眼光來看實在是非常完美的模特兒。整個聖代的尺寸很大，當作正餐來吃是一種豪華的自我獎勵呢！

Three Berry Parfait
Kajitsuen Reibell
¥2400

Perhaps the most classic topping for parfaits is the strawberry. When looking for a good strawberry parfait to paint, I discovered this parfait by Kajitsuen Reibell, and thought it was perfect. The design showcases not only the outside of the strawberry but the beautiful cross section as well, and with the additional colors of green grapes and blueberries, it really is a perfect item for food illustration. It was super big too, so it can replace a whole meal. A really luxurious treat!

（ 04 ）草莓聖代
Strawberry Parfait

APR.

4月的推薦

———— at ————

果實園里貝爾

Kajitsuen Reibell

→ 04 草莓聖代
Strawberry Parfait

1.

2.

1. 收銀檯旁的展示櫃陳列當季的高級品牌水果。　2. 很受歡迎的圓頂蛋糕可以內用也可以外帶。

1. The showcase next to the register is full of seasonal brand-name fruit. 2. The popular Zuccotto cake is available for eat in or take out.

**如果想要品嚐高級水果
一定要去水果甜點專賣店**

水果甜點專賣店是日本獨特的文化。日本有饋贈食品的習慣，這讓高品質、高單價水果得以蓬勃發展。水果甜點專賣店專門販售用這些高級水果製作成的甜點，以及能夠當作禮品的水果。我是為了吃草莓聖代才前往果實園里貝爾，但收銀檯旁的高級品牌水果也很吸引人。無論味道或外觀都經過店家嚴選，感覺水果變得好高級。

Visit fruit parlors for a taste of high-end fruit

Fruit parlors are a very uniquely Japanese concept. The culture of giving food as a gift has led to the development of very expensive, high-quality fruit. Fruit parlors are usually a combination of a fruit store and a dessert shop, and when I visited Kajitsuen Reibell, my primary goal was to eat (and then paint) a strawberry parfait; however, the brand name fruit at the counter were a great temptation as well. Fruit parlors really highlight the prestige of fruit in Japan, and I now consider fruit to be a luxury item.

看蛋糕看到入迷！

I love the look of these cakes!

蜜桃聖代

蜜桃聖代
〜搭配自製梅子醬
寇特咖啡
1600日圓

我最喜歡的甜點種類就是日本的「聖代」。不只外表非常可愛，日本的聖代基本上配料多又講究，而且還有很多原創的有趣種類。這一款聖代也是。美味的蜜桃、杏仁、朱槿果凍、優格慕斯，日向夏蜜柑*冰沙以及檸檬蛋白霜。明明是很複雜的組合，但能夠享受到各種滋味真的很棒。

※本商品為2021年限定款。
＊產自宮崎縣的柑橘品種，是宮崎有名特產。

Peach Parfait
with Homemade Plum Sauce
Coto Cafe
¥1600

My favorite category of sweets is Japanese parfaits. They are usually very visually beautiful, but it's not just the visuals alone that are appealling. They often consist of many parts, each with their own unique flavors. This parfait is a great example. Alongside the delicious peach topping was almond pudding, hibiscus gelée, yogurt mousse, citrus sherbet, and lemon merengue. While a bit complicated, it was such a treat to sample each element!

※This product was a seasonal product in 2021.

05 SHOP INFO → P042

柑橘聖代

Sun Sun Sun！

雙葉水果吧
新宿丸井本館店
1023日圓

總之整個聖代就是色彩繽紛！我為了線上
講座，刻意尋找外觀有表現張力，美味，
而且連容器都要漂亮的商品時，找到這一
款聖代。使用不只一種柑橘，綜合不同顏
色看起來非常漂亮，雕刻玻璃杯也相得益
彰。冰淇淋搭配柑橘的味道和以前常吃的
冰棒很像，是一道讓人想起童年的大人甜
點。

Sun Sun Sun!

Futaba Fruits Parlour
Shinjuku Marui Department Store
¥1023

It was so colorful! For an online class I was
developing, I wanted to find a food to paint that
was very visually exciting, as well as something
with interesting dishware. The multiple varieties
of citrus types on this parfait led to very
interesting colors, and the crystal parfait glass
was absolutely beautiful. The combination of
citrus and soft cream reminded me of a grown-
up version of the creamsicles I ate as a child.

特別版 情人節聖代

資生堂水果吧
咖啡沙龍銀座本店
2400日圓

因為想畫情人節的插圖，所以就到以聖代
聞名的資生堂水果吧去一探究竟。不過當
時正值2月，所以周遭都是情侶，雖然一
個人吃這麼大份的情人節甜點實在很不好
意思！但我還是覺得有鼓起勇氣去一趟真
是太好了。宛如美術作品般的聖代實在很
美味，是一道非常浪漫的甜品。我特別喜
歡其中加入愛心的元素！

※ 價格、商品規格皆為2022年3月底時的資訊，有
可能會變更。

1.

2.

Special Valentine Parfait

Shiseido Parlour
Ginza Head Shop "Salon de Cafe"
¥2400

I wanted to illustrate something for Valentine's
Day, and the Shiseido Parlour Valentine's Parfait
is pretty famous, so I visited the cafe in February.
All the tables around me were filled with couples, and it was honestly a bit embarrassing ordering this large Valentine's parfait by myself, but
I'm really glad I had the courage to do so. This
parfait is just a visual feast, and so very romantic.
I love the heart motifs!

※ The price and design is from March, 2022 and may
vary. Image is for illustrative purposes.

3.

1.加上香蕉的巧克力聖代1800日
圓。 2.經典又受歡迎的草莓聖
代1800日圓。 3.布丁百匯套餐
2100日圓，有附咖啡等飲品（杯
裝）。

1. Chocolate Parfait topped with a
banana ¥1800.
2. The popular and classic Strawberry Parfait ¥1800.
3. The Pudding à la Mode Set includes a drink such as coffee etc.
¥2100 (Cup Service).

喫茶店

喫茶店經常被翻譯成「咖啡廳」或「某某咖啡」，
但日本的喫茶店是不同於歐美的獨特飲食文化。
日本的喫茶店始於明治時代，模仿歐洲咖啡廳打造懷舊又古典的空間。
菜單乍看之下是西式，但仔細觀察就會發現幾乎都是歐洲風的
日本原創料理。

Kissaten is often translated to "coffee shop" or "cafe" in English,
but it is a culture all its own. First appearing in the late 1800's,
kissaten were styled after European cafes, and they retain the feeling of the old and classic.
Menu items are seemingly European, but a closer look will reveal
that they are mostly Japanese creations styled after European dishes.

08 布丁百匯
Pudding à la Mode

喫茶店的布丁百匯
特里亞農洋菓子店
803日圓

**Coffee Shop
Pudding à la Mode**
Patisserie TRIANON
¥803

法語的「a la Mode」意指「流行的」，所以「布丁百匯（Pudding a la Mode）」就是指當時最受歡迎又摩登的主流布丁甜點。包含布丁百匯在內，喫茶店菜單中經常出現的拿坡里義大利麵和燉飯，都發源自橫濱新格蘭飯店的「The Café」。在特里亞農洋菓子店可以吃到用自製的大分量布丁，搭配冰淇淋、生奶油，還有各種水果配料的經典布丁百匯喔！

"À la mode" means "in the latest fashion" in French and pudding à la mode was a "modern" take on the popular pudding. Alongside other kissaten classic menus such as napolitan pasta and doria, Hotel New Grand's "The Café" in Yokohama was the first to create pudding à la mode. At Trianon, you can eat their voluminous pudding à la mode that includes home-made pudding, ice cream, whipped cream, and fruit!

KISSATEN

08 SHOP INFO → P043

度過美好
的一天吧！
*Enjoying
lovely day!*

MAY
5月的推薦

—— at ——

特里亞農洋菓子店

Patisserie TRIANON

→ 08 布丁百匯
Pudding à la Mode

懷舊的空間令人平靜

第一次去喫茶店的時候，我一點也不了解日本的喫茶店文化，還因為老舊過時的裝潢而覺得有點驚訝。不過，在這個不斷推陳出新的世界裡，充滿懷舊風格的喫茶店格外讓人平靜。暖黃色的照明、溫暖色調的裝潢、有年代感的家具等，位於東京高圓寺的「特里亞農」讓人有種彷彿穿越到過去的感覺。除了經典的喫茶店菜單之外，還可以一邊品嚐甜點師用心製作的蛋糕，一邊享受懷舊的空間。

大片的紅色招牌就是這家店的標誌。
Look for the big red sign.

店內空間寬敞，可以在座位上舒適享用餐點。
The shop is spacious, and the table seating is quite comfortable.

店員會親切地將餐點送到桌邊。
The staff's service is warm and friendly.

隨時都有23種甜點可供外帶。
There are also 23 types of take-out desserts.

A Retro Space to Relax

When I first visited a kissaten, I had no idea about the unique culture surrounding them. In fact, I was startled by the seemingly outdated and old-fashioned interior design of these cafes. However, in a world where things update and modernize at such an extreme speed, the nostalgia that lives on in the kissaten is somehow reassuring. Yellow lighting, warm colors, and retro furniture are a staple at kissaten, and Trianon is no different. At Tokyo Koenji Trianon, in addition to delicious classic menu items, you can also enjoy a variety of cakes alongside your retro dining experience.

外觀非常可愛！
Such a cute design!

冰淇淋蘇打

Coffee Shop 戈藍

900日圓

1970年代，日本流行起結合蘇打汽水和冰淇淋的「冰淇淋蘇打」，當時冰淇淋還是非常奢侈的食物。因為哈密瓜口味廣受喜愛，而且又擁有高級感，所以奢侈的冰淇淋搭配上奢侈的哈密瓜蘇打的品項最受歡迎。雖然還有其他口味，不過鮮綠的蘇打汽水搭配紅色醃漬櫻桃已經變成經典款，幾乎所有喫茶店都會列在菜單上。

Cream Soda

Coffee Shop Gyaran

¥900

When soda with ice cream was popularized in Japan in the 1970s, ice cream was a luxury food item. As melons were also considered a luxury, the combination of melon-flavored soda and ice cream seemed like a perfect match. While other varieties of cream soda exist, the neon green color and bright red cherry are ubiquitous at kissatens across Japan.

09 SHOP INFO → P044

10 小倉吐司
Ogura Toast

吐司

銀座志川
1條（2斤）950日圓

小倉吐司是吐司搭配紅豆泥與奶油的早餐商品。因為經常看到客人把奶油吐司泡在紅豆湯裡吃，所以名古屋的喫茶店「滿葉」便發明了小倉吐司。我很想在家裡重現以前在名古屋吃過的「小倉吐司」，所以試著使用「銀座志川」厚實香甜又柔軟的正方形吐司製作。日本的吐司比歐美的更香甜，有種吃甜點的感覺，非常美味！

※插圖為作者將商品自行料理過的樣子。

Plain Bread

Ginza Nishikawa
1 Loaf ¥950

Ogura toast is a breakfast item that consists of Japanese "shokupan" bread topped with sweet beans and butter. It originated in "Kissaten Matsuba" in Nagoya, inspired by customers ordering buttered toast and dipping it in sweet bean soup. Although I first ate it on a trip to Nagoya, I wanted to try making it for myself at home. I used the sweet, fluffy, thick, and perfectly-square bread from the Ginza Nishikawa bread shop. Japanese "shokupan" is sweeter and fluffier than the western equivalent, so it makes for a dessert-like experience!

※The subject of this illustration was hand-prepared by the author.

紅豆沙

SWEET BEAN PASTE

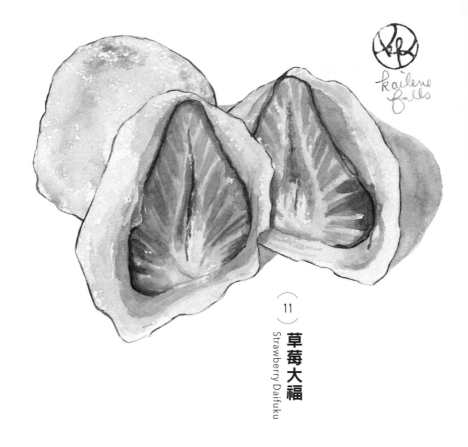

（11）
草莓大福
Strawberry Daifuku

在歐美，通常不太會把豆類做成甜食，只會做成鹹食來吃，
所以歐美人第一次吃到紅豆沙的時候或許會有點抗拒。
不過，紅豆沙是和菓子必備的食材，口感溫潤又香甜，
與各種食物搭配都很適合。

Most of the Western World only eats beans in salty dishes, so when
Westerners first eat sweetened bean paste, it takes a bit of getting used
to. However, it is one of the most important ingredients in traditional
Japanese sweets, and the unique texture combined with the sweet
flavor compliments a variety of ingredients.

品菜師的草莓大福

伊志伊

460日圓～

用紅豆沙和麻糬包覆水果的和風甜點「水果大福」之中，草莓大福最受歡迎。雖然也可用「黑豆沙」製作，但這間店為了讓客人看到草莓鮮豔的顏色，刻意使用「白豆沙」。為了讓客人不用切開大福也能看到草莓的鮮紅，很多店家都減少大福內的豆沙量。

Vegetable Sommelier Strawberry Daifuku

Ishii

From ¥460

Amongst fruit daifuku (Japanese sweets made of fruit wrapped in sweet been paste and mochi), strawberry daifuku is the most popular. While red bean paste can also be used, this shop chose to use white bean paste to better show of the bright color of the strawberries. Furthermore, they lessened the amount of bean paste at the very top so that the red of the strawberries can be easily seen through the mochi, creating a visually beautiful treat.

MAY

5月的散步

———— at ————

柴又

Shibamata

東京有很多充滿現代感的地方，但是「柴又」的街道就像穿越時空一樣，讓人可以享受古早日本的景色。有很多商家在木造建築物裡販售和風伴手禮，還有柴又帝釋天這座美麗又歷史悠久的寺院可以遊覽。

While much of Tokyo is modern, certain areas, such as Shibamata, provide a wonderful opportunity to experience the atmosphere of a traditional Japanese city. Wooden shops selling traditional souvenirs are plenty, and the famous Shibamata Taishakuten Buddhist temple is a popular tourist destination conveniently nearby.

12 餡密
Anmitsu

元祖餡蜜
銀座 若松
950日圓

東京銀座的「若松」，在1930年代發明的懷舊甜點「餡蜜」，至今仍廣受日本民眾歡迎。這道甜點使用寒天搭配水果、赤豌豆、紅豆沙、黑糖蜜，第一印象出乎意料地簡樸。不過，據說赤豌豆的事前處理非常麻煩，製作上很費工。

Original Anmitsu
Ginza Wakamatsu
¥950

Anmitsu is a retro-Japanese dessert created by the shop "Wakamatsu" in Ginza,Tokyo in the 1930s and is now a popular treat all across Japan. Made by topping agar-agar jelly with fruit, bean paste, red peas, and brown-sugar syrup, it seems like a simple dessert at first glance. However, the red peas in particular take a lot of time to prepare, and this dessert actually requires a lot of effort to make.

13 牡丹餅
Ohagi

萩餅 7 種口味組合
竹野萩餅
1900 日圓

使用白米與紅豆沙製作的甜點「萩餅」又稱「牡丹餅」。春天吃的叫做「牡丹餅」，秋天吃的叫做「萩餅」。一般的萩餅外觀都有點樸素，但是「竹野萩餅」這間店可以吃到使用南瓜、椰子、石榴、草莓等食材製作的現代化萩餅。

All Seven Types of Ohagi Set
TAKENO TO OHAGI
¥1900

Ohagi is a dessert made from rice and sweet bean paste. When eaten in the spring, this dessert is called "botamochi", and when eaten in the fall, it's called "ohagi." While traditionally a little plain in appearance, "Takeno to Ohagi" showcases a modernized version of this snack using ingredients such as pumpkin, coconut, pomegranate, and strawberries.

13 SHOP INFO → P046

法式甜點

在日本吃到的西洋甜點，比起美國，
更多是受到歐洲（主要是法國）的啟發。
日本文化自古就很重視食物的外觀，所以日本人會比較容易
接受法國人的甜點美學，這一點我很能理解。

Japan's "Western desserts" are primarily inspired by the European (particularly French) style more than the American.
Japan has a long history of placing importance on food presentation, so it is understandable that the artistic emphasis on French desserts resonates with the Japanese approach to sweets.

14 **龍貓泡芙**
Totoro Cream Puff

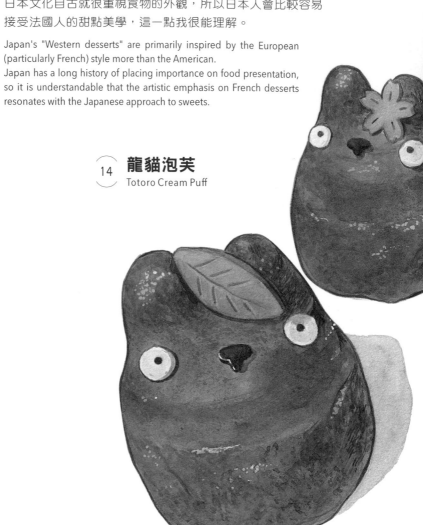

PATISSERIE

龍貓泡芙

白鬍子泡芙工房
各460〜500日圓

日本的「可愛」文化經常展現在各個地方。第一次來日本的時候，卡通人物相關產品和食物的數量多到令我吃驚。在這間位於東京・世田谷，充滿森林世界觀的咖啡店內，可以吃到全世界唯一由吉卜力認證的龍貓泡芙。因為太可愛，所以要吃掉它總覺得有點罪惡感，但真的美味到不行！

Totoro Cream Puff

Shiro-Hige's Cream Puff Factory
¥406 to ¥500 each

Japan's love of "kawaii" or "cute" things manifests itself in a variety of ways. When I first came to Japan, I was surprised at the number and variety of character-themed items, including food. Although notoriously strict about character goods, Ghibli exclusively approved these Totoro design cream puffs which can be found at this hidden treehouse-like cafe in Setagaya.

15 鮮花瑪芬
Flower Muffins

鮮花瑪芬
HANABAR
各500日圓

雖然社群媒體有不好的一面，但同時也讓我有更多機會，去發現能在漂亮空間裡享用漂亮甜點的咖啡店。HANABAR就是其中一個，這裡提供以花朵為主題的餐飲、甜點還有飲料。這裡的瑪芬不只外表漂亮，因為使用了百里香、玫瑰、荳蔻等食材，所以口味也很有趣。

Flower Muffins
HANABAR
¥500 each

While social media has many downfalls, it still gives us the opportunity to learn about beautiful cafes featuring beautiful desserts. Hanabar is just such a location with meals, bakery items, and drinks all themed around edible flowers. Their muffins aren't just pretty–they use interesting flavors such as rose, thyme, and cardamom, too.

15 SHOP INFO → **P047**

16 可麗露
Canelé

可麗露

拉・蘇爾

1個324日圓～

日本店家也很擅長把外國的傳統甜點重新發展成獨創甜點。可麗露是法國的傳統甜點，以萊姆酒與香草酒的麵糊為基底，中間像卡士達醬一樣濃稠柔軟。最近在日本非常流行。這裡不只有一般的可麗露，還有在法國找不到的抹茶、藍莓、紅茶等不同口味。

Canelé

La Soeur

From ¥324 per piece

Japan is very good at taking a classic item and making it their own. Canelé is a traditional French dessert made with rum and vanilla with a custard-like center. While anything except the traditional version is uncommon in France, Japan has made popular variations on the dessert, accented by with different ingredients such as matcha, blueberry, black tea, and a variety of other flavors.

水果丹麥麵包
Fruit Danish

黃金奇異果丹麥麵包
須藤手工烘焙
540日圓

日本的排隊文化真的很厲害。在美國我不太會去排隊，但在日本大排長龍就是美味的證明，所以我也漸漸明白，看到排隊的人龍就會情不自禁想跟著排的心情。我每次來「須藤手工烘焙」一定大排長龍，但是排隊絕對不會後悔。除了美味的鹹麵包，隨季節變化的水果丹麥麵包，奶油的香氣結合帶酸味的水果，風味亦是絕妙。

Golden Kiwi Danish
Boulangerie Sudo
¥540

When I first came to Japan, I was very surprised at the number and length of queues in Japan. However, after I lived here for a while, I realized these lines were an indicator of a great place. Nearly every time I visit Boulangerie Sudo, there is a line outside. It's for a good reason! In addition to a variety of delicious, savory breads, their seasonal danishes are both delicious and beautiful. These danishes with their buttery, layered pastry paired with tart fruit are a perfect combination.

17 SHOP INFO → P048

18 季節水果塔
Seasonal Tart

美國櫻桃水果塔

托爾斯

850日圓

在日本，使用日本櫻桃和美國櫻桃的甜點很常見。顏色比較淺的是日本櫻桃，比美國櫻桃更多汁而且較酸。根據配色和口味特色挑選使用的種類很重要。在托爾斯吃到的春季水果塔使用的是美國櫻桃，鮮奶油和奶油千層基底的比例恰到好處。

Black Cherry Tart

Torse

¥850

In Japan, there are primarily two types of cherries sold, Sakuranbo which is native to Japan, and the black cherry, called the American Cherry. Sakuranbo are lighter in color, smaller, tarter, and more juicy than black cherries, so the variety used is dependent upon the flavor profile desired. The seasonal spring tart I ate at Torse features American Cherries and uses rich cream and buttery pastry to highlight the delicious cherry flavor.

1.

JUN.
6月的購物

——— at ———

須藤手工烘焙
Boulangerie Sudo

→ (17) 水果丹麥麵包
Fruit Danish

**日本的麵包店
不會只賣原味的麵包！**

日本的甜麵包和鹹麵包文化非常有趣。不只有原味麵包，甜麵包和可以當作正餐的鹹麵包也有很多種類，餡料也都非常講究。須藤手工烘焙除了法式長棍麵包和吐司之外，也販售加入香腸、蔬菜、起司等餡料的鹹麵包，連披薩和餅乾都有，每一種都非常美味。

17 SHOP INFO → P048

看起好好吃！
Looks delicious!

2.
3.

4.

Japanese Bakeries Don't Sell Only Plain Bread!

Japan has an interesting culture of sweet breads and savory breads. Most bakeries have a strong focus on bread filled or topped with interesting ingredients. At Boulangerie Sudo, you can buy standard sandwich loaves and French bread. But what's more, you can also swing by this bakery for pizza bread, bread topped with things such as sausages, cheese, and veggies, or you can even get your hands on sweet cake-like breads and cookies.

1.麵包品項大約有60種。　2.甜點師出身的老闆親手製作的丹麥麵包品項。　3.使用當季蔬菜的披薩等可以當作正餐的麵包。　4.大受歡迎的世田谷吐司和世田山吐司，必須在開放預約日以電話預訂。

1. Around 60 varieties of bread. 2. A variety of Danishes created by a patisserie trained baker. 3. A variety of bread including pizza with seasonal veggies. 4. You can make phone reservations for the popular "Setagaya" and "Setayama" breads.

SHOP INFO

01 KIHACH甜點專賣店 東大島

パティスリー キハチ 東大島 /
PATISSERIE KIHACHI Higashi-Ojima Store

東大島
Higashi-Ojima

餐廳「KIHACHI」於1987年開業。從餐後甜點衍生出來的KIHACHI甜點專賣店，總是能提供四季最美好的滋味。

📞 03-5626-3910
📍 東京都江東区大島8-42-14
🚇 距離地鐵東大島站大島出口徒步約4分鐘

Restaurant "KIHACHI" opened in 1987. Their dessert-based patisserie delivers flavors using seasonal ingredients at their peak ripeness.

📞 +81 3-5626-3910
📍 8-42-14 Ojima, Koto-ku, Tokyo
🚇 4-min. walk from the Ojima Exit on the Higashi-Ojima Subway Station

02 Cinnabon・西雅圖貝斯特咖啡 六本木店

シナボン・シアトルズベストコーヒー 六本木店 /
Cinnabon・Seattle's Best Coffee Roppongi Store

六本木
Roppongi

1985年誕生於美國華盛頓州的西雅圖。極致講究的肉桂捲，使用特別栽種並提煉的「馬卡拉肉桂」，所以香氣十足。

📞 03-3470-4780
📍 東京都港区六本木6-5-18六本木センタービル
🚇 距離地鐵六本木站徒步約1分鐘

Established in Seattle, USA in 1985. In their cinnamon rolls, they use the highly refined and fragrant "makara cinnamon."

📞 +81 3-3470-4780
📍 Roppongi Center Building
6-5-18 Roppongi, Minato-ku, Tokyo
🚇 1-min. walk from the Roppongi Subway Station

03 簡單的夢想 日本橋別邸

かんたんなゆめ 日本橋別邸 / kantan na yume Nihonbashi Store

在已經決定要拆除的大樓落腳，只營業2年的和菓子吧。饕客可以在此搭配日本茶或日本酒，享受漂亮又具現代感的白豆沙。營業時間要上官方Instagram確認。

☎ 050-5362-1781
◎ 東京都中央区日本橋室町1-6-7 3F
Instagram: @kantan.na.yume
🚇 距離地鐵三越前站徒步約1分鐘

A Japanese wagashi bar that will be in operation for only two years until the building is demolished. You can enjoy the beautiful and modern nerikiri with Japanese tea and sake.Check Instagram for latest shop hours.

☎ +81 50-5362-1781
◎ 3F 1-6-7 Nihonbashi Muromachi, Chuo-ku, Tokyo
Instagram: @kantan.na.yume
🚇 1-min. walk from the Mitsukoshimae Subway Station

04 果實園里貝爾

果実園リーベル / Kajitsuen Reibell

持續提供正宗水果美味，超過30年以上的水果吧。從最受歡迎的水果聖代，到經過嚴選的新鮮水果，在最佳的狀態下提供給顧客。

☎ 03-6417-4740
◎ 東京都目黑區目黑1-3-16プレジデント目黑ハイツ2F
🚇 距離JR目黑站西出口徒步4分鐘

A fruit parlor that has been serving delicious fruit for over 30 years. Their desserts, including their most popular fruit parfaits, use the best fruit on the market.

☎ +81 3-6417-4740
◎ President Meguro Heights 2F
1-3-16 Meguro, Meguro-ku, Tokyo
🚇 4-min. walk from the West Exit of the JR Meguro Station

SHOP INFO

05 寇特咖啡
コトカフェ / Coto Cafe

新宿
Shinjuku

位於新宿5丁目花園神社旁的咖啡廳。如果不知道要點哪一道菜，我推薦加入無花果招牌肉凍等料理的前菜組合（600日圓～）。

📞 03-6233-7782
📍 東京都新宿区新宿5-17-6 中田ビル2F
🚶 距離各線新宿站東出口徒步8分鐘

A cafe located next to Hanazono Shrine in Shinjuku 5-chome. If you can't decide what to order, the appetizers such as the fig-filled meat patties (starting at 600 yen) are a good place to start.

📞 +81 3-6233-7782
📍 Nakata Building 2F
5-17-6 Shinjuku, Shinjuku-ku, Tokyo
🚶 8-min. walk from the East Exit of Shinjuku Station

06 雙葉水果吧 新宿丸井本館店
フタバフルーツパーラー 新宿マルイ本館店 /
Futaba Fruits Parlour Shinjuku Marui Department Store

新宿
Shinjuku

和1941年開業的水果店「雙葉水果」異業結合誕生的水果吧。店內也提供無麩質的鬆餅和純素蛋糕。

📞 03-6709-9848
📍 東京都新宿区新宿3-30-13 新宿マルイ本館 5F
🚶 距離各線新宿站東出口徒步5分鐘

A fruit parlor in collaboration with "Futaba Fruits" which was founded in 1941. They also serve vegan cakes and gluten-free pancakes.

📞 +81 3-6709-9848
📍 Shinjuku Marui Main Building 5F
3-30-13 Shinjuku, Shinjuku-ku, Tokyo
🚶 5-min. walk from the East Exit of Shinjuku Station

07 資生堂水果吧 咖啡沙龍銀座本店

資生堂パーラー 銀座本店サロン・ド・カフェ /
Shiseido Parlour Ginza Head Shop "Salon de Cafe"

銀座
Ginza

位於東京銀座資生堂大樓3樓的咖啡廳。這裡可以享用使用當季食材製作的聖代和甜點，還有傳統口味的冰淇淋蘇打。

📞 03-5537-6231（不可預約）
📍 東京都中央区銀座8-8-3 東京銀座資生堂ビル3F
🚉 距離地鐵銀座站徒步約7分鐘

A cafe on the third floor of the Tokyo Ginza Shiseido Building. You can enjoy a variety of treats included seasonal fruit desserts and ice cream floats made with same variety of soda water they have been using since 1902.

📞 +81 3-5537-6231
📍 3F Tokyo Ginza Shiseido Building
　 8-8-3 Ginza, Chuo-ku, Tokyo
🚉 7-min. walk from Ginza Subway Station

08 特里亞農洋菓子店

トリアノン洋菓子店 / Patisserie TRIANON

高圓寺
Koenji

昭和35年開業的西式糕點老店。該店的糕點師傅曾在日本蛋糕競賽獲得無數獎項。每月主題限定的造型泡芙也很受歡迎。

📞 03-3315-1451
📍 東京都杉並区高日圓寺南4-26-12
🚉 距離JR高圓寺站徒步約1分鐘

A long-established pastry shop founded in 1960. The pastry chefs here have won numerous awards at the Japan Cake Show Tokyo. Every month, they make a new variation of their popular decorated cream puff.

📞 +81 3-3315-1451
📍 4-26-12 Koenji-Minami, Suginami-ku, Tokyo
🚉 1-min. walk from JR Koenji Station

09

Coffee Shop 戈藍

Coffee Shop ギャラン / Coffee Shop Gyaran

上野
Ueno

1977年開業的老字號喫茶店。裝潢從開業以來就沒有變過，懷舊的氛圍很棒。傳統的喫茶店菜色一應俱全。

📞 03-3836-2756
📍 東京都台東区上野6-14-4-2F
🚉 距離各線上野站5b出口徒步1分鐘

A classic kissaten that opened in 1977. The interior has remained the same since opening, and the retro atmosphere is very charming. Their menu contains classic kissaten dishes and drinks.

📞 +81 3-3836-2756
📍 6-14-4 Ueno, Taito-ku, Tokyo-2F
🚉 1-min. walk from the 5b Exit of Ueno Station

10

銀座志川

銀座に志かわ / Ginza Nishikawa

銀座
Ginza

講究水質的高級吐司。麵粉使用的是加拿大產的高級品，結合嚴選奶油與鮮奶油製作。什麼都不要沾，先吃吃看原味吧。

📞 03-6263-2400
📍 東京都中央区銀座1-27-12 キャビネットビル1F
🚉 距離都營淺草線寶町站A1出口徒步4分鐘

High-quality bread that uses a very specific type of water in their recipe. They pay careful attention to the butter and fresh cream used, and even import high-end flour from Canada. Try the bread alone first before adding any extra toppings.

📞 +81 3-6263-2400
📍 Cabinet Building 1F
　 1-27-12 Ginza, Chuo-ku, Tokyo
🚉 4-min. walk from the A1 exit of Takaracho Station on the Toei Asakusa Line

11 伊志伊
い志い / Ishii

位於葛飾柴又的這間店，是帝釋天參道上最古老的建築，擁有200年的歷史。販售糕點與醃菜，長年受到顧客愛戴。可以在這裡買到別處沒有的奢侈商品，也是一種樂趣。

📞 03-3657-1749
📍 東京都葛飾区柴又7-6-20
🚃 距離京成金町線柴又站徒步約3分鐘

This store in Katsushika Shibamata is in a 200-year-old building, the oldest shop on the Taishakuten road. It has been long-loved as a store for sweets and pickles. They have a unique selection of high-quality items to enjoy.

📞 +81 3-3657-1749
📍 7-6-20 Shibamata, Katsushika-ku, Tokyo
🚃 3-min. walk from Shibamata Station on the Keisei-Kanamachi Line

12 銀座 若松
銀座若松 / Ginza Wakamatsu

這間店從明治時期傳承至今，餡蜜這道甜點的發祥地。選用十勝產紅豆與富良野產的赤豌豆，食材挑選非常講究。紅豆沙非常清爽，入口即化。

📞 03-3571-0349
📍 東京都中央区銀座5-8-20
🚃 距離地鐵銀座站徒步約3分鐘

The store that first created anmitsu in the Meiji Era (1868-1912). They are selective with ingredients, using things like azuki beans from Tokachi and red peas from Furano. Their bean paste is smooth with a pleasant mouthfeel.

📞 +81 3-3571-0349
📍 5-8-20 Ginza, Chuo-ku, Tokyo
🚃 3-min. walk from the Ginza Subway Station

13 竹野萩餅
タケノとおはぎ / TAKENO TO OHAGI

在東京都內有兩間店鋪的萩餅專賣店。花朵般的萩餅外觀非常漂亮。1天只有50組，可接受預訂。取貨點在櫻新町店。

📞 03-6413-1227
📍 東京都世田谷区桜新町1-21-11
🚃 距離東急田園都市線櫻新町站南出口徒步5分鐘

An ohagi specialty shop with two locations in Tokyo. The flower-like ohagi is very beautiful. They only sell 50 boxes a day, but you can make reservations in advance. You can pick up a box at the Sakura-Shinmachi store.

📞 +81 3-6413-1227
📍 1-21-11 Sakura-Shinmachi Setagaya-ku, Tokyo
🚃 5-min. walk from the South Exit of Sakura-Shinmachi Station on the Tokyu Den-En-Toshi Line

14 白鬍子泡芙工房
白髭のシュークリーム工房 / Shiro-Hige's Cream Puff Factory

全世界只有「白鬍子泡芙工房」可以製作「龍貓泡芙」。因為用心手工製作，所以每一隻龍貓的表情都不同。

📞 03-5787-6221
📍 東京都世田谷区代田5-3-11F
🚃 距離小田急線世田谷代田站徒步約3分鐘

The Shiro-Hige's Cream Puff Factory is the only shop in the world that makes the "Totoro Cream Puff." All of the puffs have different facial expressions, and they are baked with love.

📞 +81 3-5787-6221
📍 1F 5-3-1 Daita, Setagaya-ku, Tokyo
🚃 3-min. walk from Setagaya-Daita Station on the Odakyu Line

15 HANABAR
HANABAR

位於池袋站西出口的店家，空間充滿乾燥花，彷彿電影畫面。在這裡可以點一杯花朵雞尾酒，享受品嚐花朵的奢華時光。菜單也有花朵午餐與花朵瑪芬。

📞 03-6874-5459
📍 東京都豊島区西池袋3-30-6 磯野ビル1F
🚇 距離JR池袋站西出口徒步5分鐘

Located near the West Exit of Ikebukuro Station, this shop, filled with dried flowers, feels like a movie set. Enjoy a luxurious evening tasting flower cocktails, a flower lunch, and flower muffin.

📞 +81 3-6874-5459
📍 Isono Building 1F
3-30-6 Nishi-Ikebukuro, Toshima-ku, Tokyo
🚇 5-min. walk from the West Exit of JR Ikebukuro Station

16 拉‧蘇爾
ラ‧スール / La Soeur

源自福岡的可麗露專賣店。擁有很多搭配水果乾、堅果、巧克力等食材的原創口味。冰鎮過後再吃會有全新口感的生可麗露也很受歡迎。

📞 0570-025-888（付費電話）
📍 東京都新宿区西新宿1-1-3 小田急百貨店新宿店本館 B2F
🚇 位於各線新宿站西出口

A canelé specialty store from Fukuoka. They sell many original flavors using dried fruit, nuts and chocolate. Their "raw canelé" is eaten cold and is popular for its unique texture.

📞 +81 570-025-888
📍 Odakyu Department Store, Shinjuku Store Main Building B2F
1-1-3 Nishi-Shinjuku, Shinjuku-ku Tokyo
🚇 3-min. walk from Shinjuku Station

17 須藤手工烘焙
ブーランジェリースドウ / Boulangerie Sudo

世田谷
Setagaya

位於世田谷線松陰神社前站的麵包糕點店。特製的的現烤麵包，還有季節限定的西式糕點都不容錯過。

📞 03-5426-0175
📍 東京都世田谷区世田谷4-3-14
🏠 距離世田谷線松陰神社前站徒步約1分鐘

A bread and baked sweets shop located in front of Shoin-Jinja-Mae Station on the Setagaya Line. Don't miss their specialty breads and seasonal pastries.

📞 +81 3-5426-0175
📍 4-3-14 Setagaya, Setagaya-ku, Tokyo
🏠 1-min. walk from the Shoin-Jinja-Mae Station on the Setagaya Line

18 托爾斯
トルス / Torse

祐天寺
Yutenji

時光緩緩流逝的咖啡店。蛋包飯和咖哩飯等正餐累積了眾多粉絲，還有自家精心製作的甜點與飲料。

📞 03-6453-2418
📍 東京都世田谷区下馬5-35-5
🏠 距離東急東橫線祐天寺站徒步約13分鐘

A cafe to visit for a relaxing experience. Their meals, such as omurice and curry, have many fans. Their special homemade sweets and drinks are also popular.

+81 3-6453-2418
5-35-5 Shimouma, Setagaya-ku, Tokyo
13-min. walk from Yutenji Station on the Tokyu Toyoko line

PART 1

參考照片的
拍攝祕訣

Tips for Taking Good Reference Photos

要畫寫實風格的插畫，參考照片是作品成敗的關鍵，所以我建議要自己拍攝。這裡分享一些拍攝食物插畫參考照片的祕訣！

When painting realistically, the reference image is half of the final piece. Therefore, I always recommend taking your own references when you can! Here are some tips.

1　以白色為背景拍攝照片。水彩是畫在白色的紙上，所以參考照片如果也是白色背景，就能畫出自然的光影和反射色。我的包包裡隨時都攜帶能夠當作照片背景的白紙。

2　選擇配色好看的食物。炸物等顏色比較平淡的食物，可以加上香草、蔬菜或者用盤子來營造跳色。

3　注意想傳達的重點再決定拍攝角度。譬如說，採俯視的角度會比較容易看清楚每個細節，但就不容易呈現立體感。從側面拍攝的話，雖然不容易看清楚每個細節，但相對容易呈現立體感。

4　幫照片加工也OK！把色調和構圖調整到滿意為止吧！

1　Try to take the reference image against a white background. This way, the shadows and colors reflected on the food won't look awkward when illustrated on a white piece of paper. I always bring a sheet of white paper with me whenever I visit restaurants.

2　Choose food that has good colors. If the food itself has only one color (like fried food) try to include accent colors with side items like herbs, vegetables, or even the dishware.

3　Consider what you want to convey then decide the angle. Certain angles will convey different things: from above will showcase all parts of the dish well, but the food will look more flat. At a 3/4s angle, the food will look very dimensional, but some parts may be hidden.

4　Don't be afraid to edit the photo with apps. Adjust the layout and colors until you are happy the with results!

7
月
8
月

SUMMER

July

August

日本的夏天雖然濕度高，
但是可以用刨冰等冰涼的食物來撐過炎炎酷暑。
而且夏天有很多街頭小吃，
尤其是祭典可以吃到的美食，我最喜歡了！

Japan's summer is very humid, but cold treats like shaved ice
help me get through these hot days.
Festivals and street food also offer a lot of delicious options
during the summer months!

經典日本美食

CLASSIC JAPANESE FOODS

日本料理多到數不完，國外日本料理食譜一定會出現的
菜色只占其中一小部分而已。
無論出現的歷史長短，這個類別的食物在喜歡日本料理
的外國人眼中，都是很知名的菜色。

While there is a wide variety of traditional food in Japan, there are
certain dishes that nearly always appear in international Japanese
cookbooks. Whether the history of these dishes is long or short,
they have become well-known to Japanese food
enthusiasts thoughout the world.

⌒ 19 ⌣ 拉麵
Ramen

柚子醬油拉麵
AFURI
1080日圓

據說拉麵從中國傳來，1900年代初期才第一次在日本登場。直到1950年代，拉麵都被稱為「中華麵」，至今仍有店家使用這個稱呼。然而，日本拉麵的調味和中國不同，進化成日本特有的料理。這間店使用加入柚子的醬油湯底，味道很有日本風格。

Yuzu (Citrus) Soy Sauce Ramen
AFURI
¥1080

Ramen first appeared in Japan in the early 1900s and was imported from China. Until the 1950s, it was called "Chinese soba," and you can still find some shops today that sell it under that name. Despite this, Japanese ramen has developed its own unique combination of flavors and toppings, different from its Chinese counterpart. This ramen had a soy sauce base with a yuzu accent, a very Japanese combination.

20 炸豬排
Tonkatsu (Pork Cutlet)

特製炸里肌豬排定食（300ｇ）
炸豬排檍
2000日圓

西式料理剛開始傳到日本的時候，日本
廚師將其改造成對日本人來說好親近又
合口味的菜式。「炸豬排」就是源自將
牛肉煎烤過的「法式肉排」。將牛肉改
為在日本比較容易取得的豬肉，麵包
屑用麵包粉代替，便誕生炸豬排這道
菜。順帶一提，之所以搭配高麗菜一
起吃，據說是因為高麗菜富含維他
命，可以幫助消化炸豬排的油膩。

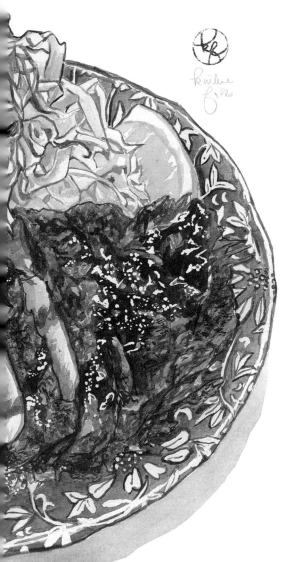

Special Pork Cutlet Meal(300g)

Tonkatsu Aoki

¥2000

When Western cuisine first came to Japan, Japanese chefs tried to reinvent it to make it more accessible and enjoyable to the Japanese palate. Tonkatsu is a Japanese take on "côtelette de veau," a French dish of caramelized, roasted beef. By changing it to the more accessible pork and replacing the breadcrumbs for panko, the Japanese classic tonkatsu was born. Interestingly, tonkatsu is almost always served with cabbage, as the vitamins found in it help with digesting the fattiness of the fried pork.

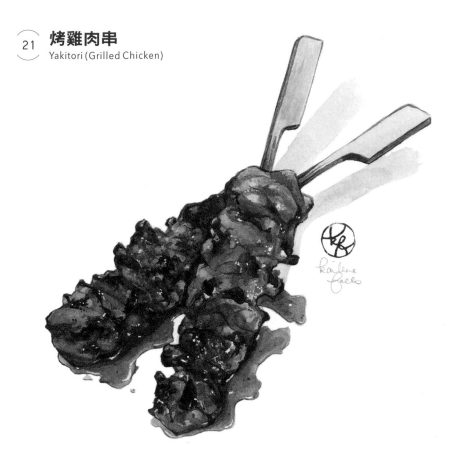

炭火烤雞肉串 雞腿肉（醬燒）
全家便利商店
130 日圓

烤雞肉串是一種用竹籤串起雞肉，再用炭火烤過的料理。經常使用雞胸、雞腿、雞肝、雞皮、雞心等部位來製作。通常使用鹽巴或醬汁調味，在串烤店、便利商店、祭典路邊攤、居酒屋都能吃到。這裡畫的是便利商店買的醬燒烤雞肉串，為了讓視覺效果更好，所以額外購買其他店家的醬汁，謹慎地淋上。

※此為 2022 年 4 月 1 日的價格

Charcoal-Grilled Chicken Thigh Meat (Sauce Flavor)
Family Mart
¥130

Yakitori, or "grilled chicken," is skewered pieces of charcoal-grilled chicken. Common yakitori includes anything from breast and thigh meat to liver, skin, and heart. It can be served salted or with sauce, and is found at shops called "yakitori-ya," convenience stores, festivals, and izakaya pubs. This yakitori from the convenience store was "sauce flavored," so when I styled the food for this piece, I decided to carefully add extra sauce splatters to convey the flavor.

※Current price as of April 1st, 2022.

21 SHOP INFO → P091

22 炸雞塊
Kara-Age (Fried Chicken)

名菜！入味炸雞塊
爸爸吃炸雞塊，我吃義大利麵
3塊330日圓

炸雞是廣受全世界喜愛的料理。日本的
「炸雞塊」使用無骨雞腿肉，以日式風格
的調味（醬油、酒、生薑等），再沾上太
白粉與麵粉下鍋油炸。美國沒有太白粉，
大多使用玉米粉，我覺得日本的炸雞塊吃
起來比較酥脆。這間店同時提供炸雞和義
大利麵，該店也委託我畫了暖簾的插圖。

Specialty! Fried Chicken
Papa wa Kara-Age, Watashi wa Pasta
3 pieces ¥330

Fried chicken is popular around the world, and each country has their own style. Japan's "kara-age" is hard to resist with its small cuts of flavorful thigh meat. Most kara-age are marinated in soy sauce, sake, and ginger before being coated in potato starch and flour and then deep fried. While Western chicken is often made with corn starch, the potato starch in kara-age has a crispier texture. I illustrated the signage for this shop featuring a variety of Japanese kara-age and pasta dishes.

23 飯糰
Onigiri (Rice Ball)

究極生筋子*

飯糰屋On
620日圓

據推測，「飯糰」從彌生時代就有了。平安時期的貴族設宴待客時，會在庭院發飯糰給僕人吃。1700年左右就出現的海苔飯糰，直到現在依然經常被拿來當早餐或帶便當，野餐、賞花等場合也會吃到。在「飯糰屋On」可以買到嚴選食材的極品飯糰。

*被卵巢薄膜包覆的魚卵。

Ultimate Sujiko

Onigiriya On
¥620

Remains of formed balls of rice have been found dating back to the Yayoi Period (300 BC to 300 AD), and in the Heian Period, rice balls were given as gifts to servants as tokens of appreciation. The modern version, wrapped in nori seaweed, first appeared in the 1700s and still continue to be eaten today as easy breakfast and lunch items. They are also a popular portable food eaten at flower-viewing parties and picnics.

24 涼拌豆腐
Hiyayakko (Cold Tofu)

絹豆腐
太田屋豆腐店
180日圓

豆腐是源自中國的食物，奈良時代傳來日本，尤其不吃肉類和魚類的僧侶經常食用。至今在東京的住宅區，像「太田屋豆腐店」這種小型豆腐店仍然很常見。「涼拌豆腐」不需要加熱，只要加上生薑、蔥花、柴魚、茗荷、醬油等調味就可以完成，是一道簡單的豆腐料理。

※插圖為作者將商品自行料理過的樣子。

Silken Tofu
Ootaya Tofu Shop
¥180

Originally coming to Japan via China during the Nara Period (710-784 AD), tofu became quite popular as an ingredient as it was friendly to the Buddhist vegetarian diet. Nowadays, you can find many neighborhood mom-and-pop shops in Tokyo like "Ootaya Tofu Shop" selling homemade tofu. Hiyayakko is a popular and simple preparation using ginger, green onions, bonito flakes, myoga, and soy sauce as toppings on uncooked silken tofu.

※The subject of this illustration was hand-prepared by the author.

1.以不輾壓米飯的力道，輕巧快速地捏飯糰。　2.餡料是從全日本各地蒐羅的嚴選食材。3.客人點餐後才開始製作，所以吃到的都是現做的飯糰。

1. Working quickly so that the rice texture isn't compromised. 2. All the fillings were carefully selected from across Japan. 3. The onigiri is made to order so it's always fresh.

1.

2.

3.

JUL.
7月的推薦

———— at ————

飯糰屋 On

Onigiriya On

→ 23 飯糰
Onigiri (Rice Ball)

飯糰充滿母親的愛

日本的流行料理「飯糰」，是在熱騰騰的飯裡加入喜歡的餡料，然後用沾著鹽巴的手捏成形。作法、食材都很簡單。正因為如此，「飯糰屋On」顯得對食材非常講究。「究極生筋子」使用的是稀少、難以取得的阿拉斯加產紅鮭魚的生筋子。白米、食鹽、海苔等所有食材，都是店主花了好幾年的時間從全日本各地嚴選來的。即便價格稍貴，也貴得有道理。

23 SHOP INFO → P092

5.

6.

4.大受歡迎的究極生筋子口味620日圓、鮭魚口味290日圓。店內販售約有20種飯糰。　5.有很多常客是追隨老闆澤井而來。　6.店面外觀是位於十字路口的一棟白色建築物。

4. The popular "Ultimate Sujiko" for 620 yen, and the Salmon for 290 yen. There are roughly 20 varieties of onirigiri for sale. 5. Many customers come to interact with the owner, Sawai-san. 6. The shop is the white building at the corner of the inter-section.

4.

Onigiri Made with a Mother's Love

The popular Japanese food "onigiri" is made by forming warm, salted rice into balls and then filling or topping them with various ingredients. The technique and ingredients are simple. Therefore, "Onigiriya On," is very particular about the quality of the ingredients. The "Ultimate Sujiko" rice ball is made with the eggs of the elusive Alaskan wild trout. Rice, salt, seaweed: all the ingredients were hand-selected by the owner who sourced them after many years of travelling around Japan. These onigiri are definitely worth the slightly steeper price tag.

隨時歡迎各位光臨！
Stop by anytime!

有趣的
吃法與作法

在美國，很少有餐廳是讓客人在座位上自己料理，
我覺得這是很棒的日本文化。
和朋友一起去這種餐廳吃飯很好玩，即便是和不太熟的人一起去，
動手做也能成為話題，讓大家變得更親近。

In America, cook-at-your-table style restaurants are quite uncommon, but in Japan, they are a part of popular culture. Not only are they are a lot of fun to visit with friends, they are also a great place to visit with new acquaintances. Cooking together can lead to interesting conversations and help people become closer to each other.

UNUSUAL PREPARATIONS /
DINING EXPERIENCES

在鐵板上煎大阪燒。用金屬製的鍋鏟切開，然後移到盤子上享用。不知道怎麼料理時，店員會教你。

Okonomiyaki is cooked on a tabletop grill. It's eaten after cutting it with a metal spatula and dividing it onto plates. If you're not sure how to make it, the staff can show you!

25 大阪燒
Okonomiyaki

綜合天
Teppan職人
1380日圓

大阪燒是大阪的名產。在歐美，不太會有餐廳把烤盤直接放在餐桌上，所以第一次吃大阪燒的時，我覺得非常新鮮。大阪燒的經典口味是調味醬、美乃滋、海苔粉再加上柴魚片。宛如在跳舞般的輕薄柴魚片讓我很驚喜，完全擄獲我的心。

Mixed Ten
Teppan Shokunin
¥1380

Okonomiyaki is a dish originating in Osaka. Tabletop grills are rather unusual in the Western World, so the experience of preparing okonomiyaki at your own table was new and exciting for me. The most classic version of this dish is topped with sauce, mayonaise, nori, and bonito flakes, and because bonito flakes are so thin, they react to the heat and air from the grill and look almost like they are dancing on top of the okonomiyaki!

來試著做吧！ *Let's make some monja!*

店員會教你怎麼做。
The staff taught me how to prepare monjayaki.

首先把料倒出來，用鍋鏟劃碎。
First, put the solid ingredients on the grill and chop them up.

把餡料圍成圓圈，然後在正中間倒入高湯麵糊。
Next, make a ring with the solid ingredients and pour the liquid in the center.

起司麻糬明太子文字燒

近藤文字燒 總店

1580日圓

文字燒也會使用鐵板,但不是大阪風格,而是東京風格。作法比大阪燒稍微難一點,不像鬆餅那樣有厚度,而是薄薄地攤開成一大片,然後用小鏟子從邊緣一點一點慢慢吃,這種吃法非常有趣。這間店位於傳說中文字燒發源地的月島,也是這裡歷史最悠久的商家,原本是一間賣零食的店。據說,以前孩子們會從家裡帶來各種食材,請店家做成文字燒。

Mochi Cheese Mentaiko Monja

Monja Kondo Head Shop

¥1580

Monjayaki is another dish prepared on a grill at your own table. It is considered to be Tokyo's version of okonomiyaki, but unlike its Osakan counterpart, it isn't formed into a pancake. Instead, after being spread out thinly and cooked on the grill, a tiny spatula is used to scrape away at the cooked edges to eat a little at a time. This monjayaki is from the oldest shop in Tsukishima, the birthplace of monjayaki. While the shop used to sell candy, it turned into a monja shop where children would bring their own ingredients from home for the shop master to use as monjayaki toppings.

再等一下就完成了!
Almost done!

好好吃!
Delicious!

料和高湯麵糊混合後,薄薄地開。

hen, mix the solid and liquid arts together and spread thinly n the grill.

煎好後從邊緣剷起來吃。

Finally, once it's cooked, scrape off a bit at a time with a spatula and eat.

因為太美味了,忍不住笑出來。

So yummy it puts a smile on my face!

27 涮涮鍋
Shabu-Shabu

Let Us 豪華套餐
Let Us 涮涮鍋 中目黑總店
2000 日圓

說到我最喜歡的日本料理，可能就
是涮涮鍋了。涮涮鍋這個名稱的來
源也很有趣。大阪有一間叫做「末
廣」的餐廳，在思考這道菜的菜名
時，因為員工用水盆洗擦手巾的聲
音和涮肉的聲音很像，所以取名
為Shabu-Shabu。我喜歡昆布高
湯、豆漿高湯，還有微辣口味的高
湯。

Premium Let Us Set
Shabu Shabu Let Us
Nakameguro Head Store
¥2000

Shabu-Shabu is probably my favorite
Japanese food. Also originating in
Osaka, the dish was apparently named
when the shop owner heard the sound
of the wet hand towels (o"shabu"ri)
being washed in a basin and realized it
was similar to how you swish meat and
vegetables in broth for this dish. In
addition to classic kombu broth, I'm also
a big fan of soy milk and spicy broths.

27 SHOP INFO → P094

JUL.
7月的推薦

—— at ——

Let Us 涮涮鍋
中目黑總店

Shabu-Shabu Let Us
Nakameguro Head Store

→ (27) 涮涮鍋
Shabu-Shabu

1.

2.

3.

一個人也可以享受涮涮鍋的美味

我明明超喜歡涮涮鍋，可是一年吃不到幾次。因為大鍋需要幾個人分食，所以人數不夠就沒辦法吃。然而，位於東京中目黑的「Let Us」是單人鍋專賣店，這對我來說真是一大福音。使用小尺寸的湯鍋，每個座位都有瓦斯爐，一個人也能享受涮涮鍋。在時尚的空間裡，蔬菜擺盤顯得特別豪華。

Shabu-Shabu
That Can Be Enjoyed Alone

Despite being one of my very favorite Japanese foods, shabu-shabu is a dish that I only eat a few times a year. Most restaurants serve it family-style, with a large pot of broth shared at the table. However, I was very excited when I heard about the shabu-shabu at Let Us in Meguro, Tokyo, because they specialize in one-person ser-vings. Using smaller pots and individual stovetops at each seat, individual eaters can enjoy the food and experience without visiting with a whole group. The vibe inside the shop is modern Japanese, with careful attention paid to the displays of ingredients.

1.涮涮鍋使用當季的美味蔬菜。契作的農家會從日本各地寄送過來。　2.綜合蔬菜擺盤非常漂亮。　3.總共有超過29種醬汁和豐富的調味料，可以按照自己的喜好搭配。

1. Enjoy seasonal vegetables with your shabu-shabu. The shop has contracts with farmers across Japan who directly ship them their stock. 2. A beautiful display of the vegetable plates. 3. From dipping sauces to condiments, you can create your own flavor combination from 29 different ingredients.

27 SHOP INFO → P094

輕輕涮過肉片～
"Shabu-shabu"
that meat!

4.

好美味!
Delicious!

5.

4.一人一鍋，可以在自己喜歡的時間點享用真的好開心。肉類涮過2～3次，當肉片變成粉紅色就可以吃了。小心不要把肉涮過頭，會變得很老喔！　5.除了一般座位，還有吧檯的座位。

4. With a single-serving pot, you can eat shabu-shabu whenever you like. Swish the meat back and forth two to three times, and when the meat turns subtly pink, it's time to eat. Don't let the meat get tough! 5. In addition to table seating, there is also counter seating.

我在美國明尼蘇達州出生，節慶時可以吃到用竹籤串起來的食物，雖然種類是有名的豐富，不過以油炸食物居多。來日本之後發現有很多非油炸的品項，讓我很驚奇；而且不僅限於節慶的時候，只要去觀光景點，就有很多商品可以選擇。

My home state of Minnesota prides itself on the huge variety of "foods on sticks" at their state fairs. However foods on sticks in theUSA usually consist of fried foods, so when I came to Japan, I was surprised at the number of non-fried foods on sticks here. They aren't just limited to festivals either and can often be found at famous tourist spots to be enjoyed while sightseeing.

28 築地的玉子燒
Tsukiji Omelet

串玉
築地 山長
100日圓

Kushi Tama
Tsukiji Yamachou
¥100

在便當裡面會吃到的玉子燒通常沒有串起來，但築地 山長的玉子燒不一樣，用竹籤串著可以邊走邊吃。這間店是排隊名店，排隊的時候能看到師傅製作玉子燒的過程。店內販售的玉子燒有「甜」和「不甜」兩種口味，我個人喜歡砂糖和食鹽調和出有層次的甜口味。

Although tamagoyaki is often served in bento boxes without sticks, "Yamachou's omelets on sticks are both delicious and a convenient way to eat while exploring Tsukiji's outer market. People line up outside, and while in line you can watch them make the eggs on the spot. They sell both sweet and unsweetened tamagoyaki, but I am a big fan of the sweet and savory flavor of the dashi version.

JUL.

7 月的推薦

— at —

築地場外市場

Tsukiji Outer Market

1.

2.

3.

除了吃海鮮、買海鮮！
築地名產玉子燒也很推薦

我第一次來日本的時候，築地是日本最大的魚市場。市場內會進行拍賣，只有業內的師傅才能入場，但場外市場有很多餐廳讓一般民眾也能享用美味魚料理。雖然魚市場已經移到豐洲，但場外市場仍然是可以享用美味魚料理的人氣商圈。我剛開始這麼想：「魚市場中的人氣料理怎麼會是玉子燒？」感覺魚市場和玉子燒不太搭，原來這道料理使用的是魚高湯。無論何時都有人為了它大排長龍。

1.築地場外有很多魚販，可以採購新鮮的漁獲。 2.在「築地 山長」能看到玉子燒的製作過程。 3.請拿起雞蛋捲串，大口咬下吧！

1. Tsukiji's Outer Market has many fish shops where you can buy fresh seafood. 2. Tamagoyaki being made at Tsukiji Yamachou. 3. You can eat the tamagoyaki directly off the stick!

When Buying and Eating Seafood at the Market, Don't Miss the Famous Tsukiji Omelets!

When I first came to Tokyo, Tsukiji Market was the largest fish market in Japan. It was split into two — the inner market where auctions and wholesale occurred, and the outer market where tourists and regular people could buy delicious foods. While the inner market has now moved to Toyosu, the outer market of Tsukiji is still open and is quite a popular place to eat both seafood and a wide variety of street food. While seemingly out of place at first, Japanese omelets use a seafood based stock in their egg mixture, and the omelets at Yamachou always have a long line of people eager to eat them.

鹽烤山女鱒

這道鹽烤料理使用的是日本淡水魚「山女鱒」。攤位在靠近日光國立公園的瀑布附近。外觀有點奇怪，所以我一開始有點敬而遠之，但是想到難得來一趟就吃吃看吧。雖然骨頭多不太方便吃，但食鹽與微焦的魚香味很搭。

Shioyaki (Salt-Grilled) Yamame Trout

This shioyaki is made with a Japanese freshwater trout called "Yamame." I ate it at a street food stall near the waterfalls at Nikko National Park. It looked a little grotesque, so I had never wanted to eat it before, but I gave it a try anyways. The fish was freshly caught, and although it was a little hard to eat around the bones, the salt and char accented the flavor really well.

五平餅

一般來說「餅」是用糯米搗至麻糬狀的料理。然而「五平餅」使用的不是糯米，而是梗米。梗米搗碎後用竹籤串起來，淋上調味醬汁，用炭火烤至出現香味為止。我是在東京青山明治神宮外苑的攤販那吃到的。

Gohei Mochi

Mochi is usually made from sticky rice that is pounded until it becomes sticky and dough-like material. Gohei mochi is unique in that it is made with non-sticky rice. Once pounded into a cake, it is skewered, coated with sauce, and aromatically grilled over an open flame. I ate this gohei mochi at Meiji-Jingu Gaien in the Aoyama district of Tokyo.

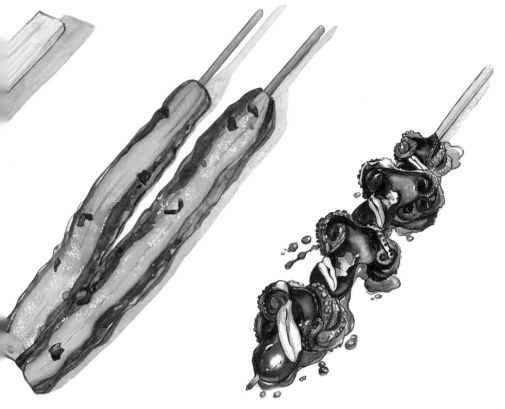

醃小黃瓜

去參加祭典我一定會吃醃小黃瓜。因為實在太喜歡，非夏季也會想吃，所以在網路上找了食譜自己做。和美國的醃黃瓜相比，日本的醃漬食品比較新鮮、口感細緻，我一個人也能輕鬆吃掉兩支醃小黃瓜。

Whole Pickled Cucumber

Pickled cucumbers on sticks are one of my must-have festival foods. Sometimes I crave them during off-seasons, so I found a recipe online to make my own. Compared to American pickles, Japanese pickles are much fresher and subtler in flavor, and I can actually eat two whole cucumbers by myself.

短爪章魚

我第一次在淺草的路邊攤看到短爪章魚的串烤，覺得外觀非常不可思議。不過味道我很喜歡！我有好長一段時間都以為這是「日本的人氣攤販料理」，但其實短爪章魚串烤有點罕見。

Iidako

When I first saw iidako (tiny octopuses) on sticks at a street food stand by Sensoji Temple, they seemed very strange. But I loved the flavor! For years, I mistakenly thought this was a common Japanese snack, but I later learned it is actually pretty rare.

透明金魚飴細工

飴細工 吉原

1620日圓

飴細工是用麥芽糖做出動物或花朵等形狀的日本傳統技藝。明明有數百年的歷史，但飴細工師傅卻只有寥寥數人。雖然有顏色的麥芽糖很多，但我個人覺得透明色特別漂亮，就像美術品一樣。

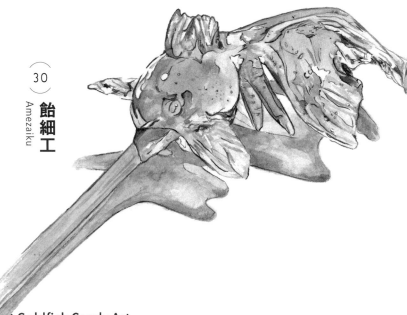

（30）飴細工 Amezaiku

Transparent Goldfish Candy Art

Amezaiku Yoshihara

¥1620

Amezaiku, or "candy artistry," is a traditional Japanese craft of sculpting candy into intricate shapes such as flowers, animals, etc. Although it has been around for hundreds of years, it is said that only a handful of artists still practice the craft. There are transparent and apaque-colored versions, but I personally love the artistic look of the transparent candies the most.

特製蘋果糖
原味
Pomme d'Amour 東京

648日圓

蘋果糖是1908年由美國的糖果製造商威廉・科爾布發明的商品。不過，中國、歐洲各國自古都有水果淋上糖漿的吃法，所以日本的「蘋果糖」究竟源於哪裡，其實很難斷定。這間店一整年都能吃到原味和搭配各種配料的蘋果糖。

31

Candy Apple

蘋果糖

Pomme d'Amour
Special Candied Apple - Plain
POMME d'AMOUR TOKYO

¥648

Candied apples were invented in 1908 by an American candy maker named William W. Kolb. However, candied fruit is traditional in China and other Asian countries, so it's hard to say if the "ringo ame" found in Japan are inspired by the American treat or by other Asian confections. At this shop, you can try both classic and fancy candied apples all year long.

我很喜歡畫有透明感的食物。
透明處的顏色和光影反射很有趣，
這種素材本來就很適合透明度高的水彩畫。
日本有很多透明的食物，本篇只能介紹其中一部分。

Transparent foods are one of my very favorite things to paint.
The way colors and reflections behave in transparent foods is very unique and
interesting, and watercolor, being an inherently transparent medium,
is the perfect tool for recreating these colors. Japan has a number of transparent foods,
and this category features just a small sampling.

32 繡球花冰淇淋蘇打
Hydrangea Float

繡球花冰淇淋蘇打
Sunday Brunch 下北澤店
980 日圓

我最喜歡的花就是繡球花。我美國祖
父母家附近有很多繡球花，在我來日
本之前不知道繡球花是亞洲的花。6
月繡球花開時，也會出現很多繡球花
甜點，這一點很符合日本的風格。這
款冰淇淋蘇打使用藍色和紫色的果凍
表現繡球花的概念。

※這是4月中旬～6月底的限定商品。

Hydrangea Float
Sunday Brunch Shimo-Kitazawa Shop
¥980

My favorite flower is the hydrangea. My
grandparents' neighborhood in the US had
many hydrangea plants, but I didn't know
they were an Asian flower until I came to
Japan and discovered how plentiful they
are here. And in a very Japanese fashion,
hydrangea-themed foods pop up during
June. This cream soda uses purple and
blue gelatin to represent the colorful
bunches of hydrangea flowers.

※This is a limited menu item from mid-April to end
of June.

32 SHOP INFO → P096

刨冰

藍色夏威夷刨冰

明水亭

400日圓

「藍色夏威夷」到底是什麼味道？其實口
味不固定！有蘇打、蜜桃、萊姆等各種
不同的滋味，但外觀都是顯眼的藍色。儘
管如此，在祭典等場合上經常可以看到對
吧！這是在吉祥寺井之頭恩賜公園找到的
藍色夏威夷刨冰。冰涼又清爽的味道，非
常適合夏天。

Blue Hawaii Shaved Ice

Meisuitei

¥400

What does blue Hawaii flavor taste like? Actually,
the flavor itself isn't set – some taste like soda,
some like peach, some like ramune soda, etc.
There are a number of variations, and the only
thing they have in common is their bright blue
color. Despite this, it is a popular item found
at many summer festivals in Japan. This little
shop in Inokashira Park in Kichijoji sells blue
Hawaiian shaved ice, and the refreshing cold
treat is perfect for summer!

33 SHOP INFO → P096

蜂蜜檸檬與都路里冰

茶寮都路里 大丸東京店

1419日圓／1463日圓

刨冰原本是在祭典時能夠以親民價格購買的甜點，但是現在刨冰文化已經往更高級的方向進化了。使用水果、麻糬、紅豆沙等各種配料，讓刨冰成為奢華的夏日甜品。在辻利吃到的抹茶、蜂蜜檸檬刨冰，豪華的滋味令人難以忘懷。

※ 刨冰為5月中旬～9月下旬的限定商品。插圖為以
　 前的商品示意圖。有可能會變更。

Honey Lemon & Tsujiri Shaved Ice

Saryo Tsujiri Daimaru Tokyo Shop

¥1419 / ¥1463

While shaved ice has traditionally been a relatively cheap treat to eat at festivals, in recent years, Japan has begun topping shaved ice with extravagant toppings to make them a more deluxe dessert. Toppings like mochi, fruit, and red bean paste are just the tip of the iceberg. These fancy shaved ices from Tsujiri featured ice made from matcha as well as a honey-lemon shaved ice, a popular summer flavor in Japan.

※ Shaved ice is available for a limited time from mid-May
　 to late September.

33 SHOP INFO → P097

AUG.

8月的回憶

— at —

井之頭恩賜公園

Inokashira Park

→ (33) 刨冰
Shaved Ice

**不必參加祭典，
在公園吃刨冰也能擁有祭典的氛圍**

井之頭恩賜公園很適合在這裡度過一整天的時光。既能享受大自然，也能搭乘池塘裡的小船，還有漂亮的寺院等適合拍美照的景點。公園內也有小巧可愛的咖啡店和商店。明水亭是一間可以買到零食、懷舊蘇打、經典刨冰等商品的店家。最近除了有祭典的地方之外，很少看到店家販售刨冰，不過這間店在夏季隨時都能吃到刨冰喔。

33 SHOP INFO → P096

位於公園中央「井之頭池」中的天鵝
船、能量景點「井之頭辯才天（大盛
寺）」、小商店「明水亭」的外觀。園內
占地寬廣，很適合散步。

Rentable swan boats in Inokashira Pond, located
in the center of the park. You can also find the
Inokashira Benzaiten (Daiseiji Temple) and the
Meisuitei shop. The park is very large and perfect
for walking.

稍微休息一下！
Take a little break!

Even Without the Festival, You Can Enjoy a Festival-Shaved-Ice at the Park.

Inokashira Part is a beautiful place to spend a day.
You can enjoy scenic nature, ride boats on the pond,
and visit some beautiful temples. that make for
great photos. In addition, there are a few little shops
and cafes that border the park. Meisuitei is a tiny
shop that sells traditional candy, drinks, and classic
shaved ice. Simple-style shaved ice is usually only
found at festivals, but a trip to the park can satisfy
your craving all summer long.

34 錦玉羹
Kingyokukan

季節上生菓子*6顆裝禮盒

和菓 三納

約3000日圓

Seasonal Raw Japanese Confection Box - 6 Pieces

Wanoka Sannou

About ¥3000

和菓子大多會配合季節製作。其中讓我一見鍾情的甜點就是「錦玉羹」。將寒天融於水中，加入砂糖燉煮，待冷卻後凝固，就是夏季經典的生菓子了。「和菓 三納」的錦玉羹使用寒天果凍的透明感來表現水的感覺，裡面加入金魚造型的果凍，外觀非常漂亮。

* 生菓子指含水量較高，水分達30％以上的和菓子，上生菓子則是指上等的生菓子，由師傅根據季節設計、手工製作，不耐久放，食用期限為1～2日。

Many traditional Japanese sweets are very seasonal. Amongst these sweets, I immediately fell in love with the visual of "kingyokukan," A classic, Japanese dessert, it's made of chilled agar-agar, water, and sugar. Wanoka Sanno uses transparent blue agar-agar jelly to represent water and fish-shaped jellies to float in the "pond," making a beautiful summer dessert.

PENNY CANDY

販售零食的柑仔店源自江戶時代。

據說當時低價販售使用黑砂糖和澱粉糖漿製作的零食，以取代使用高級白砂糖的「上菓子」。讓日本人懷念的柑仔店在1950～1980年代達到頂峰，不過現在很遺憾已越來越少了。

Early versions of dagashi (penny candy) shops first appeared in the Edo Period.
They sold cheaper candy made of brown sugar or sugar syrup in replacement
of the more expensive white sugar candy that artisans sold.
Dagashi shops were very popular in the 1950s to 1980s,
but unfortunately there are only a few still left today.

35 彈珠汽水與零食
Ramune & Dagashi (Penny Candy)

彈珠汽水與零食
上川口屋
牛奶糖76日圓、彈珠汽水140日圓、彈珠汽水糖54日圓、香魚片22日圓

彈珠汽水獨具特色的瓶身發源自英國。因為軟木塞成本高又容易漏氣，所以才想到利用碳酸本身的氣壓，以彈珠為瓶蓋做設計。以前曾經廣受全世界歡迎，但現在除了日本的彈珠汽水，沒有其他商品使用這種包裝。插圖為彈珠汽水（飲料）、彈珠汽水糖（零食）、牛奶糖、香魚片。

Ramune & Dagashi (Penny Candies)
Kamikawaguchiya
Millky ¥76 / Ramune ¥140 / Ramune Candies ¥54 / Dried Fish Cake ¥22

At nearly all dagashi shops, you can find a version of ramune. The unique bottles were originally invented in England. Cork was expensive and carbonation would go flat with cork-stopped bottles, so the ramune bottles used the pressure from the soda's carbonation to seal a marble on top in place of a cap. Although these bottles were once popular around the world, Japan's ramune is one of the few products that still use it today. For this illustration, I painted ramune (the drink), ramune candies, Milky candies, and a dried fish cake.

上：雜司谷站附近的雜司谷鬼子母神堂。　下：位於神堂境內一隅的小建築物就是上川口屋。深受當地小孩和大人們喜愛。

Above:Zoshigaya Kishimojin-Do near Zoshigaya Station.
Below:The small building located on the temple grounds is Kamikawaguchiya. It's loved by all the local children and adults.

→ 〔35〕 彈珠汽水與零食
Ramune & Dagashi (Penny Candies)

在懷舊的柑仔店體驗
令人懷念的日本

上川口屋是東京尚在營業中的柑仔店裡，歷史最悠久的一間。地點就在供奉安產、育兒之神——鬼子母神的雜司谷鬼子母神堂的旁邊。由於是超過80歲的老奶奶經營，所以營業時間不固定，不過在開店的時候去一趟，一定會是非常棒的體驗。這是一間可以用低廉的價格購買懷舊零食和飲料，還能感受到漫長歷史的商店。

Experience Nostalgic Japan
at a Retro Candy Store

Kamikawaguchiya is Tokyo's oldest dagashi (penny candy) shop still in business. It is located adjacent to the Kishimojin Temple which is dedicated to the Buddhist diety who protects and cares for children. The shop is currently run by an elderly lady in her 80s, so the hours are a bit eratic, but if you can find the right time to visit, you're in for a real treat. Retro candies and snacks can be purchased very cheaply, and you can feel the history of the shop as you browse the selection.

35 SHOP INFO → P098

1781年開業。據說從江戶時代就開始營業。
店頭陳列超過100種以上的零食，每一種都
想買。

Built in 1781 and in business since the Edo
Period. There are over 100 varieties of snacks
and candies arranged for sale, and you'll be
tempted by them all.

要選哪一個呢？

What should I buy?

決定買彈珠汽水！

I got a
ramune soda!

36

嘎哩嘎哩君剉冰棒
Gari Gari kun

嘎哩嘎哩君剉冰棒 蘇打口味
赤城乳業株式會社
76日圓

1981年誕生的「嘎哩嘎哩君剉冰棒」經
常在日本的漫畫和動畫等各種流行文化中
出現。口感內層和外層不同是一大特色，
除了整年都可以買到的蘇打口味之外，其
實還有很多不同的口味。以前曾經販售過
奇異果和咖啡等聽起來很好吃的口味，也
推出過需要勇氣挑戰的奶油燉菜和煎蛋捲
等有點奇特的口味。

Gari Gari Kun Soda Flavor
Akagi Nyugyo Co., Ltd.
¥76

"Gari Gari Kun" popsicles were invented in
1981 making many appearances in Japanese
pop culture such as anime and manga. The
double texture is smooth on the outside and
crushed on the inside. Aside from the classic
soda flavor, the company has created a large
number of flavors such as kiwi or coffee, as well
as more challenging flavors like cream stew and
fried egg.

37 噴嘰布丁
Putchin Pudding

Big 噴嘰布丁 160g

江崎格力高股份有限公司

Big：125日圓左右

歐洲和南美有「法蘭」這種偏硬的布丁，而美國的布丁則是像優格一樣綿軟，因此第一次吃到日本的布丁時，我大受震撼。於1970年代商品化的噴嘰布丁，最大的特徵就是花朵般的容器。據說名稱源自只要按壓一下杯底突出處，「噴嘰」一聲就能輕鬆把布丁推出來。

Big Puchin Pudding 160g

Ezaki Glico Co., Ltd.

Big: Around ¥125

Although the stiffer "flan" is popular in Europe and South America, American pudding tends to be very soft and yogurt-like, so when I first encountered Japan's stiffer pudding, I was quite surprised. Pucchin Pudding became a product in the 1970s, and the unique flower shape makes it very recognizable. The bottom of the package has a small tab, so when you place the container upside down and break the tab, the release of pressure allows the pudding to fall neatly from the package onto a plate. The name "Puchin" comes from the sound of the tab breaking.

kailene falls

SHOP INFO

19 AFURI
AFURI

惠比壽
Ebisu

閃耀金黃色光澤的湯底，就是拉麵的生命。高湯使用位於神奈川縣丹澤山系通稱阿夫利山的天然礦泉水。這間店最具代表的品項就是「柚子鹽拉麵」。

📞 03-5795-0750
📍 東京都渋谷区恵比寿1-1-7 117ビル1F
🚉 距離JR惠比壽站徒步約3分鐘

The golden-colored soup is the soul of this ramen. They source natural water from Mt. Afuri, a mountain within the more commonly known Tanzawa Mountain Range in Kanagawa Prefecture. Their specialty is their "Yuzu Shio Ramen."

📞 +81 3-5795-0750
📍 117 Building 1F
   1-1-7 Ebisu, Shibuya-ku, Tokyo
🚉 3-min. walk from the JR Ebisu Station

20 炸豬排檍
とんかつ檍 / Tonkatsu Aoki

蒲田
Kamata

使用油脂豐富美味的「林SPF」豬肉。店內提供肉質柔嫩、油脂甘甜、肉汁豐富的頂級炸豬排。美味到即便是排隊也在所不惜。

📞 03-3739-4231
📍 東京都大田区蒲田5-43-7
🚉 距離JR蒲田站西出口徒步4分鐘

Their dishes use "Hayashi SPF" pork with delicious fattiness. They provide high-grade pork cutlets with tender, juicy meat and sweet fat. The taste is well worth the wait in line.

📞 +81 3-3739-4231
📍 5-43-7 Kamata, Ota-ku, Tokyo
🚉 4-min. walk from the East Exit of the JR Kamata Station

全家便利商店
Family Mart

目標是與當地居民成為一家人的便利商店。收銀櫃旁的中式肉包系列和全家炸雞等熱食，每一樣都美味到讓人吃了會上癮。

📞 0120-079-188（總公司）
📍 東京都內約有2400間分店，日本國內總共有1萬6570間分店。

A convenience store that aims to be your "local family." The display next to the register features Chinese steamed buns and hot snacks like Famichiki, all of which are addictively delicious.

📞 +81 120-079-188
📍 About 2,400 stores in Tokyo / about 16,570 stores in Japan

爸爸吃炸雞塊，我吃義大利麵
パパは唐揚げ、私はパスタ /
Papa wa Kara-Age, Watashi wa Pasta

糀谷
Kojiya

蒲田的「木偶奇遇義大利麵」和「東京炸雞舞」合作推出的店家。有著柔嫩多汁的炸雞和極致講究的生義大利麵＊兩種料理。

＊ 生義大利麵比起市面販售的義大利麵少了烘烤這道程序，無法久放，通常指新鮮現做的義大利麵。

📞 070-8550-0731
📍 東京都大田区萩中1-6-9 OKビル1F
🚉 距離京急糀谷站徒步約3分鐘

A collaboration shop between "Pastabar Don Pinocchio" and "Tokyo Kara-age Mai" in Kamata. Soft and juicy fried chicken and fresh pasta with the perfect texture.

📞 +81 70-8550-0731
📍 OK Building 1F
1-6-9 Haginaka, Ota-ku, Tokyo
🚉 3-min. walk from the Keikyu Kojiya Station

23 飯糰屋 On
おにぎりや On / Onigiriya On

用賀
Yoga

選用石川縣白山六星農場特別栽種的越光米，搭配嚴選白米、海苔、食鹽、配料，打造廣受歡迎的飯糰。

📞 03-3708-3336
📍 東京都世田谷区玉川台2-36-12 1F
🚇 距離東急田園都市縣用賀站徒步5分鐘

Rice balls that give you the energy for your day by combining seaweed, salt, and other ingredients to compliment the specially-cultivated Koshihikari rice produced by Rokusei Farm in Hakusan, Ishikawa Prefecture.

📞 +81 3-3708-3336
📍 1F 2-36-12 Tamagawadai, Setagaya-ku, Tokyo
🚇 5-min. walk from Yoga Station on the Tokyu Den-En-Toshi Line

24 太田屋豆腐店
太田屋豆腐店 / Ootaya Tofu Shop

代代木上原
Yoyogi-Uehara

在代代木上原擁有將近90年歷史的豆腐老店。現在的老闆是第3代。廣受當地居民喜愛的豆漿也很推薦。

📞 03-3467-2365
📍 東京都渋谷区上原1-22-5
🚇 距離小田急線代代木上原站徒步約3分鐘

A long-established tofu shop in Yoyogi-Uehara with a history of nearly 90 years. The current head is the third generation to run the shop. Their highly-recommended soy milk is also loved by the locals.

📞 +81 3-3467-2365
📍 1-22-5 Uehara, Shibuya-ku, Tokyo
🚇 3-min. walk from Yoyogi-Uehara Station on the Odakyu Line

25 Teppan 職人

Teppan 職人 / Teppan Shokunin

距離錦糸町南出口只要步行30秒就能抵達。提供大阪燒、文字燒、鐵板燒等豐富的商品。由專業的師傅現場料理，欣賞料理過程也是一種享受。

📞 03-3846-3102
📍 東京都墨田区江東橋3-12-5 マスカットビル3F
🚇 距離JR錦糸町站南出口徒步1分鐘

Located a 30-second walk from Kinshicho South Exit. They offer a wide variety of okonomiyaki, monjayaki, and teppanyaki. Professional craftsmen will cook it in front of you while you enjoy the show.

📞 +81 3-3846-3102
📍 Muscat Building 3F
3-12-5 Kotobashi, Sumida-ku, Tokyo
🚇 4-min. walk from the South Exit of the JR Kinshicho Station

26 近藤文字燒 總店

もんじゃ近どう 本店 / Monja Kondo Head Shop

昭和25年開業。戰後不久就在柑仔店的一隅販售文字燒。我個人推薦配料豐富的近藤特製文字燒（1540日圓）。

📞 03-3533-4555
📍 東京都中央区月島3-12-10
🚇 距離地鐵月島站5號出口徒步5分鐘

Founded as a candy shop in 1950. Shortly after the war, they started grilling monjayaki in a corner of their candy store. Their "Special Kondo Monja" (¥1540) is filled with lots of ingredients and comes highly recommended.

📞 +81 3-3533-4555
📍 3-12-10 Tsukishima, Chuo-ku, Tokyo
🚇 5-min. walk from the 5 Exit of Tsukishima Subway Station

27 Let Us 涮涮鍋 中目黑總店

しゃぶしゃぶ れたす 中目黒本店 /
Shabu Shabu Let Us Nakameguro Head Store

中目黑
Nakameguro

以一人一鍋十人十鍋為概念，推出嶄新型態的涮涮鍋專賣店。在充滿手作感的舒適空間裡，無論是單人或是團體都能享受「一人一鍋」的服務。

📞 03-6451-2920
📍 東京都目黑区上目黑2-12-1
　　Rootus Nakamguro 2F
🚇 距離地鐵中目黑站徒步約2分鐘

A shabu-shabu specialty restaurant with a unique concept: one person, one pot; ten people, ten pots. The vibe is relaxing with a hand-made touch to the interior design. It is always "one person, one pot," even if you visit as a group.

📞 +81 3-6451-2920
📍 Rootus Nakamguro 2F
　　2-12-1 Kami-Meguro, Meguro-ku, Tokyo
🚇 2-min. walk from the Naka-Meguro Subway Station

28 築地 山長

築地 山長 / Tsukiji Yamachou

築地
Tsukiji

昭和24年開業，位於築地的玉子燒專賣店。繼承傳統的高湯，日日用心煎好每一份商品的頂級玉子燒。1/3尺寸280日圓起。

📞 03-3248-6002
📍 東京都中央区築地4-10-10
🚇 距離都營大江戶線築地市場站徒步約3分鐘

Tsukiji's tamagoyaki specialty store was founded in 1949. Their high-quality tamagoyaki are made with a traditional soup stock recipe passed down through generations and are individually grilled with love every day. The 1/3 cut size starts at ¥280.

📞 +81 3-3248-6002
📍 4-10-10 Tsukiji, Chuo-ku, Tokyo
🚇 3-min. walk from Tsukijishio Station on the Toei Oedo Line

30 飴細工 吉原

あめ細工 吉原 / Amezaiku Yoshihara

這是日本第一家專營「日本傳統工藝飴細工」常設路面店。千駄木總店自古以來，所販售的商品都是現場手工製作，谷中店工作坊則會舉辦飴細工體驗會。

📞 03-6323-3319
◎ 東京都文京区千駄木1-23-5 巴ビル1F
🚻 距離地鐵千駄木站徒步約2分鐘

Japan's first permanent store specializing in Japanese traditional candy work. The Sendagi head shop sells candy and holds demonstrations of their old-fashioned techniques. The Yanaka location holds candy art workshops.

📞 +81 3-6323-3319
◎ Tomoe Building 1F
　 1-23-5 Sendagi, Bunkyo-ku, Tokyo
🚻 2-min. walk from the Sendagi Subway Station

31 POMME d'AMOUR 東京

ポムダムールトーキョー / POMME d'AMOUR TOKYO

據說這是日本第一家蘋果糖專賣店。在這裡你可以充分享受懷舊又閃亮亮的美麗蘋果糖魅力。剛開始請先嘗試最受歡迎的原味蘋果糖（660日圓）。

📞 03-6380-1194
◎ 東京都新宿区新宿5-9-12 KIビル2F
🚻 距離地鐵新宿三丁目站徒步約4分鐘

Japan's first candy apple specialty store. You can enjoy the charm of a nostalgic and beautiful candied apple. Start with the most popular plain version (660 yen).

📞 +81 3-6380-1194
◎ KI Building 2F
　 5-9-12 Shinjuku, Shinjuku-ku, Tokyo
🚻 4-min. walk from the Shinjuku-Sanchome Subway Station

32 Sunday Brunch 下北澤店

サンデーブランチ下北沢店 /
Sunday Brunch Shimo-Kitazawa Shop

下北澤
Shimo-Kitazawa

在這裡可以享受到以講究的法式吐司、當季蔬果製作的正餐與甜點。在溫和的陽光與綠意包圍下，度過特別的咖啡時光。

📞 03-5453-3366
📍 東京都世田谷区北沢2-29-2 フェニキアビル 2F
🚻 距離小田急線下北澤站徒步約2分鐘

A pleasant cafe experience where you can enjoy being surrounded by greenery and natural light. Be sure to try their skillfully prepared French toast or meals/sweets made with seasonal vegetables and fruit.

📞 +81 3-5453-3366
📍 Phenicia Building 2F
   2-29-2 Kitazawa, Setagaya-ku, Tokyo
🚻 3-min. walk from the Shimo-Kitazawa Station on the Odakyu Line

33 明水亭

明水亭 / Meisuitei

吉祥寺
Kichijoji

位於井之頭恩賜公園內的商店。知名商品為熱狗餃子400日圓。店內備有糯米丸、零食、啤酒、果汁等各種商品，很適合在這裡歇腳休息。

📞 無
📍 東京都三鷹市井の頭4-1-9
🚻 距離JR吉祥寺站徒步約6分鐘

A shop within Inokashira Park. Their specialty is the "Dumpling Dog" for 400 yen. Swing by and enjoy a break with various items such as dumplings, sweets, beer, and juice.

📞 Unavailable
📍 4-1-9 Inokashira, Mitaka City, Tokyo
🚻 6-min. walk from the JR Kichijoji Station

33 茶寮都路里 大丸東京店

茶寮都路里 大丸東京店 / Saryo Tsujiri Daimaru Tokyo Shop

宇治茶專賣店「祇園辻利」推出的甜品店。在能
感受到京都・祇園風情的空間中，享用宇治茶、
抹茶甜點。

📞 03-3214-3322
📍 東京都千代田区丸の内1-9-1 大丸東京店 10F
🚉 距離JR東京站徒步約2分鐘

A sweets shop produced by Gion Tsujiri, an uji tea
specialty store. You can enjoy uji tea and matcha
sweets in a space created to feel like a cafe in Gion,
Kyoto.

📞 +81 3-3214-3322
📍 Daimaru Tokyo store 10F
　　1-9-1 Marunouchi, Chiyoda-ku, Tokyo
🚉 2-min. walk from the JR Tokyo Station

34 和菓 三納

和の菓 さんのう / Wanoka Sanno

Instagram 帳號6.8萬人追蹤，在國外也具知名
度的和菓子創作家三納寬之主理的店面。可以在
社群媒體上確認販售商品的最新資訊。

📞 無
HP: https://wanoka-sanno.com
Instagram: @wagashi_sanchan

The shop owned by Hiroyuki Sanno, a Japanese
sweets creator who has more than 68,000 followers
on Instagram and is active overseas. Check updates
on social media for product information.

📞 Unavailable
Homepage: https://wanoka-sanno.com
Instagram: @wagashi_sanchan

35 上川口屋
上川口屋 / Kamikawaguchiya

位於鬼子母堂境內的柑仔店。自江戶時代就營業至今，開業超過 240 年。這裡有販售 10 日圓就能買到的零食，煩惱要選哪一種也很令人開心。

📞 03-3980-9779
📍 東京都豐島区雑司ヶ谷3-15-20鬼子母神境內
🚇 距離地鐵雑司谷站徒步約2分鐘

A penny-candy shop on the grounds of Kishimojin Temple. Established in the Edo Period, it has been in business for over 240 years. It's fun to choose which sweets you can buy starting at only ¥10.

📞 +81 3-3980-9779
📍 Whithin Kishimojin Temple Grounds 3-15-20 Zoshigaya, Toshima-ku, Tokyo
🚇 2-min. walk from the Zoshigaya Subway Station

36 赤城乳業株式會社
赤城乳業株式会社 / Akagi Nyugyo Co., Ltd.

因為嘎哩嘎哩君剉冰棒而廣受大眾所知的冰淇淋專營製造商。總公司位於琦玉縣深谷市。非常重視玩心，持續製作充滿夢想的冰淇淋產品。

📞 0120-571-591（客服專線）
📍 購買請至便利商店或各大超市

An ice cream manufacturer most known for their "Gari Gari Kun" popsicles. The head office is located in Fukaya City in Saitama Prefecture. They value playfulness in their products and continue to make ice creams "full of dreams."

📞 +81 120-571-591
📍 Convenience Stores and Supermarkets

37 江崎格力高股份有限公司

江崎グリコ株式会社 / Ezaki Glico Co., Ltd.

以「日日健康，人生豐富」為宗旨，製作出百力滋和 Pocky 等大家都知道的零食。2022 年迎來開業 100 年的大日子。

☎ 06-6477-8352（總公司）
◎ 購買請至便利商店或各大超市

A food manufacturer that makes well-known snacks such as Pretz and Pocky, based on the motto "Healthy Days, Rich Lives." The year 2022 marked the 100th anniversary of its founding.

☎ +81 6-6477-8352
◎ Convenience Stores and Supermarkets

要吃什麼好呢？

*What should
I eat?*

9　10　11
月　月　月

AUTUMN

September

October

November

有別於我出生的地方，日本的秋季長達數月。
有好多以竹筍、柿子、南瓜等食材入菜的美味料理，
所以我最喜歡在秋日散步回程的時候探訪新店家。

Unlike where I grew up, fall weather lasts many months in Japan.
Delicious ingredients like mushroom, persimmon,
and pumpkin make for comforting fall dishes.
It's the perfect season for long walks to discover new restaurants.

據說日本第一間洋食＊專賣店是1863年在長崎開業的「良林亭」。
主廚以外國的食譜為基礎，把食材換成在日本容易取得、日本人又吃得慣
的食物。許多洋食外觀很像外國料理，容易讓人誤會，但其實是在日本創
作的菜式。

Japan's first restaurant specializing in Western food "Ryourintei" opened
in Nagasaki in 1863. As Western food grew in popularity, chefs began creating recipes
inspired by foreign dishes but altered with more easily accessible ingredients
that better suited the Japanese palate. While these foods may seem to be
Western dishes, they are all Japanese in origin.

＊洋食指傳到日本後，經日本本土化的西洋餐點，即日式西餐。

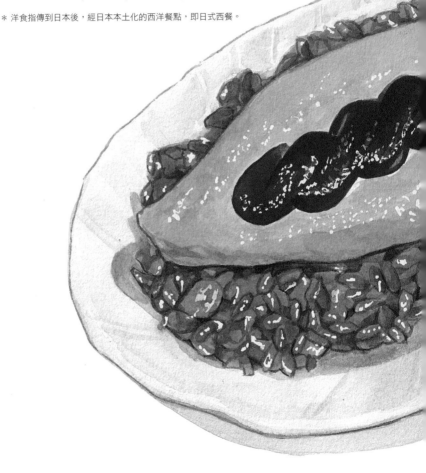

38 蛋包飯
Omurice

蛋包飯套餐 (附飲料)
喫茶 YOU
1300日圓

有好幾家餐廳都被說是蛋包飯的始祖，其中最有名的就是東京‧銀座的「煉瓦亭」和大阪‧心齋橋的「北極星」。菜名用外來語標示，「歐姆蛋」加上「飯」就成了「蛋包飯」。有別於外國的歐姆蛋，日本的蛋包飯會把外層煎熟，但中間保持濃稠蛋液的口感，切開的時候視覺效果很好。

Omurice Set(With Drink)

Cafe YOU
¥1300

The true origin of omurice is debated, as multiple shops claim to have invented it, the most famous being "Rengatei" in Ginza, Tokyo and "Hokkyokusei" in Shinsaibashi, Osaka. The name is a combination of two foreign words: "omelet" and "rice." Unlike most Western omelets however, most omurice chefs use a technique that cooks the egg more thoroughly on the outside while leaving the center quite soft and still liquid. This allows for an interesting visual when the omelet is cut open.

39 拿坡里義大利麵
Napolitan Pasta

拿坡里義大利麵 外加荷包蛋

Pancho 義大利麵 澀谷店

860日圓

拿坡里義大利麵誕生於1950年，據說是受到駐紮在日本的美軍所食用的番茄紅醬義大利麵啟發製作而成。當時番茄紅醬還未在日本普及，所以用日本人熟悉的番茄醬取代。明明是從美國傳來在日本發展的一道菜，卻用義大利的城鎮「拿坡里」命名為「拿坡里義大利麵」。加上一顆荷包蛋的Pancho義大利麵，視覺效果看起來很豐盛！

Napolitan (Regular Size) with Fried Eg

Spaghetti no Pancho Shibuya Shop

¥860

Napolitan was invented in the 1950s. The chef was inspired by the tomato sauce pasta dishes that the US military members ate while they were based in Japan. However, since tomato sauce wasn't commonly found in Japan, he decided to use ketchup which was already quite popular. He named the dish after Naples, Italy, despite the dish being a Japanese invention. One of the Napolitan pastas at "Spaghetti no Pancho" includes a fried egg on top which makes for a great visual impact.

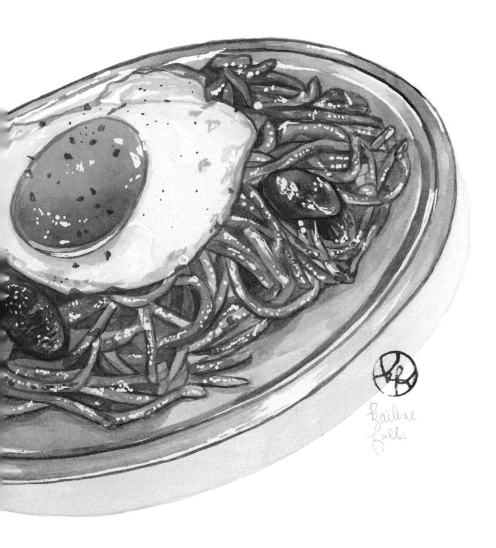

A特餐（炸里肌肉＆炸蝦）

炸物亭
1045日圓

銀座的「煉瓦亭」在1900年設計出炸蝦
這道菜。當時，炸豬排很受歡迎，所以店
家嘗試把各種食材裹上麵包粉油炸，結果
發現天婦羅的品項裡面最受歡迎的就是炸
蝦。炸豬排店「炸物亭」的人氣午餐，
炸蝦與炸里肌肉的套餐採用現炸的方式製
作，麵包粉酥酥脆脆的口感真的非常美
味。

Lunch Set A
(Pork Cutlet and Fried Shrimp)

Fry Tei
¥1045

Deep-fried, breaded shrimp was first invented
by a chef in Renga-tei, a Western food
restaurant in Ginza. Seeing the popularity of
pork cutlets, the shop attempted to bread other
foods, eventually landing on shrimp as a good
option since it was already popular for tempura.
Thus was born Japanese fried shrimp. The
breading on the fried shrimp and pork cutlet at
"Fry Tei" was nice and crisp, and the flavor was
really satisfying.

40 SHOP INFO → P143

41 鱈魚子義大利麵
Tarako Spaghetti

**醃漬魚卵與真鯛的奢華
「頂級鱈魚子」義大利麵**

義大利麵＆紅酒 壁之穴
1980日圓

日本的主廚非常擅長在西洋料理中使用日
式食材。鱈魚子義大利麵就是在西洋食物
義大利麵與橄欖油中，加入日本人最喜歡
的鱈魚子、魚卵、海苔、芥末、紫蘇等食
材，完成一道天才般的料理。提供紅酒與
和風義大利麵的「壁之穴」是發明鱈魚子
義大利麵的餐廳，義大利麵上還搭配魚
卵，看起來非常豪華！

※現在餐點內容已有所變動。

Luxury 'Best Tarako' Spaghetti with Salmon Roe and Red Sea Bream

Pasta & Wine Kabe no Ana
¥1980

Japanese chefs are skilled at creating fusion
foods combining Japanese and Western
ingredients. Tarako pasta combines pasta and
olive oil with a variety of Japanese ingredients
such as cod roe, salmon roe, nori seaweed,
wasabi, and shiso leaves. This wine and pasta
shop "Kabe no Ana" was the inventor of tarako
pasta. Their pasta, with the addition of the
salmon roe is really a treat.

※The current menu may differ.

42 吉野家的牛丼
Yoshinoya's Gyudon

旅遊書大多不會介紹連鎖店。

大家往往會認為連鎖店全日本都有，而且菜單也沒有獨創性。

不過透過連鎖店可以了解一個國家的文化和國民的喜好，這一點非常有趣。

本篇將為各位介紹非常美味又令人印象深刻的日本連鎖店。

Travel guides often overlook chain restaurants as they are perceived as commonplace and not unique. However, they often are quite specific to each country, with different types of food and menus clearly showcasing cultural preferences. Here are a few chain restaurants that made an impact on me in Japan.

蔥花雞蛋牛丼

吉野家

中碗 544 日圓

日本直到明治時代初期都禁止國民吃牛肉。自明治5年（1872年）解禁到受大眾歡迎花了不少時間，而吉野家創業於明治32年（1899年），已經算是非常早了。現在日本國內外累計有超過2000間以上的分店正在營業中。

※ 價格皆為2022年3月時的定價。

Negi Tama Gyudon (Green Onion and Egg Beef Bowl)

Yoshinoya

Regular Size ¥544

Eating beef was banned in Japan until the early Meiji Period. After the ban was lifted in 1872, it took time for beef to become popular, but Yoshinoya was one of the earliest beef specialty shops to open in Japan in 1899. Now it functions as a Japanese-style fast food restaurant with over 2,000 different locations worldwide.

※Information is current as of March 2022.

這一道也很受歡迎！ **This is popular, too!**

吉野家經典的中碗牛丼426日圓。牛肉、洋蔥、白米等所有食材都經過嚴選的良品。

Yoshinoya's classic dish, Regular-Size Gyudon for ¥425. Beef, onion, rice, etc., everything is carefully prepared.

牛肉壽喜鍋中碗712日圓。冬季限定菜單。有大片的壽喜燒肉以及白菜等大量蔬菜。

The Regular-Size Gyu-Suki Nabe for ¥712, only available during the winter. Filled with large cuts of sukiyaki meat, chinese cabbage, and other vegetables.

CoCo壹番屋的咖哩飯
CoCoICHI's Curry Rice

炸里肌咖哩
加蔬菜

CoCo壹番屋咖哩

1095日圓

咖哩原本是印度料理，但在日本的咖哩
則是經過一番波折才產生。印度曾經被
英國統治，英國船員把咖哩帶回自己的
家鄉改良，之後又傳進日本，再度改良
過一次。相較於印度咖哩，日本的咖哩
口味偏甜，使用蘋果、蜂蜜等印度不會
使用的食材，也會加入肉類。因為口味
偏甜，所以在日本連小孩子都喜歡吃咖
哩。

※部分地區價格有所不同。

Pork Cutlet Curry with Vegetables

CURRY HOUSE CoCoICHIBANYA

¥1095

While curry is originally an Indian dish, it
arrived to Japan via British ships. British
sailors had already altered Indian curry by
making it thicker and sweeter than the
Indian version, and Japanese chefs altered it
even further, using ingredients like apples
and honey, and adding different meats and
vegetables as toppings. The sweet flavor
makes it a popular dish across Japan, even
amongst children.

※Prices may differ by region.

這一道也很受歡迎！ **This is popular, too!**

波菜咖哩779日圓。加上富含鐵質
與維他命C的波菜，很受注重健康
的族群歡迎。

Spinach Curry for ¥779. Topped
with iron and vitamin-c-filled
spinach. Popular amongst the
health-conscience customers.

香腸咖哩853日圓。大人小孩都
喜歡的香腸。香腸肉有著香甜與
Q彈的口感，令人食指大動。

Sausage Curry for 853 yen.
Sausage is popular with both
children and adults. The umami-
packed meat with the snappy
texture is irresist-able.

來一份客製咖哩吧！
Don't forget to customize!

咖哩醬5種、配料約40種、辣度從普通開始有11個等級、甜度有6個等級，可以自由選擇。排列組合全部總共約有2億種。

Choose from five kinds of curry sauces, 40 types of toppings, 11 levels of spiciness, and add additional sweetness up to level six. If you tried every combo, there would be roughly 200,000,000 varieties.

SEP.

9月最喜歡的事

— at —

CoCo 壹番屋

CoCoICHI

→ ㊸ 壹番的咖哩飯
CoCoICHI's Curry Rice

從咖哩醬到配菜都可以有各種搭配，真的好開心！

有別於國外的餐廳，日本的餐飲店很少會換菜單，也很少提供客製化服務。因此，第一次去CoCo壹番屋的時候，我很驚訝他們的服務風格。雖然有標準的菜單，但是可以改變咖哩的辣度、甜度，還有約40種配料和5種咖哩醬可以選擇，任何人都能訂製符合自己口味的咖哩。

又辣又美味！
Spicy and delicious!

日本最受歡迎的餐點是炸里肌咖哩864日圓，外加蔬菜231日圓。據說在美國的分店，最受歡迎的是炸雞咖哩。

The most popular curry: Roast Cutlet Curry for ¥864, topped with vegetables for an extra ¥231. In America, the most popular topping is chicken cutlet.

You can customize everything from the sauce to the toppings!

Most restaurants in Japan offer food as-is, with very little customization allowed. When I first visited CoCo ICHIBANYA, I was very surprised at their style of service. Besides ordering a standard menu item, customers can also to alter the style of sauce, the spiciness, the sweetness, and even add their choice of toppings. With around 40 different toppings and five different sauces, nearly everyone can find a version of curry to suit their preference.

44 **麥當勞的
季節限定漢堡**
McDonald's Seasonal Burger

月見起司堡

麥當勞

370日圓（2021年）

麥當勞1955年在美國開業，1971年在
日本開了第一間分店，販售像是大麥克
與炸薯條等和美國一樣的商品。但比起
這些，日本限定的菜單更為有趣，我都
會推薦給來自外國的觀光客。照燒麥克
堡和秋季限定的月見漢堡*等充滿日本
風情的商品我特別喜歡。

※ 由於是期間限定的商品，目前不一定有販售。
＊ 牛肉漢堡排、煙燻培根，搭配蛋白蛋黃分明的
　圓形月見蛋，是日本麥當勞搭配中秋節上市的
　經典秋季商品。

Cheese Tsukimi

McDonald's

¥370(2021)

McDonald's was founded in 1955 in the
USA, and in 1971, they opened their first
shop in Japan. While many menu items such
as the Big Mac and french fries are nearly
identical to the American menu, Japan's
other menu items are something all visitors
to Japan should try. Items like the Teriyaki
Mac Burger or the autumn-limited-time
Tsukimi (Moon Viewing) Burger really
showcase Japanese flavors.

※This is a seasonal menu item and is not currently for sale.

這一道
也很受
歡迎！ **This is popular, too!**

照燒麥克堡350日圓。將豬肉排以日
本特有的甜辣「照燒醬汁」調味，是
烤肉風格的絕妙滋味。

The Teriyaki Mac Burger for 350 yen.
A pork patty topped with an authentic
Japanese teriyaki-flavored, sweet and
spicy sauce.

炸蝦堡®390日圓。加入大量蝦肉的
酥脆炸蝦排與極光醬非常搭。

The Shrimp Filet-O for 390 yen. A
crispy cutlet filled with shrimp and the
delicious aurora sauce make the
perfect combination.

這裡的「第一」不是「最好」的意思。
然而，能夠持續經營數十年的店家，本身就是美味的證據。
接下來要介紹在日本大受歡迎的國民美食，
我將分享據說是最初發明的幾家店。

First doesn't always mean best. However, when the first restaurant to make something is still popular decades later, you know that their food has to be good. Here are a few restaurants that claim their fame by being the first to create a popular Japanese food.

銅鑼燒
兔屋
1個230日圓

銅鑼燒的麵糊是蜂蜜蛋糕，而蜂蜜蛋糕是受到葡萄牙商人帶進日本的蛋糕所啟發而製作出來的。銅鑼燒的「銅鑼」是打擊樂器，這個單字有個非常有趣的傳說。武將源義經逃往奧州的時候，銅鑼就留在當地，那面銅鑼後來被當成鐵板拿來煎麵糊，所以才會取名為「銅鑼燒」。

Dorayaki
USAGIYA
1 piece ¥230

The bread on dorayaki is made from castella, a Japanese cake inspired by treats brought to Japan by Portugeuse merchants. "Dora" means "gong," and there is an interesting legend about how dorayaki got its name. When the samurai Minamoto no Yoshitsune fled to Oshu, he left behind a gong. That gong was later used in place of an iron grill to cook dorayaki.

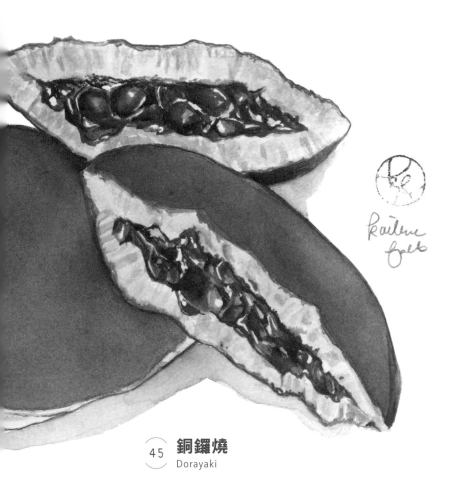

45 銅鑼燒
Dorayaki

1.

2.

3.

4.

OCT.
10月的推薦

— at —

兔 屋

USAGIYA

→ (45) 銅鑼燒
Dorayaki

**擁有百年以上的歷史
處處講究的銅鑼燒！**

以前的銅鑼燒只有紅豆沙和一片餅皮而已，現在兩片餅皮的銅鑼燒是在1925年左右才由「兔屋」初次商品化。同時使用以前的老方法與新技術，每一次都能製作出完美的銅鑼燒。明明是和菓子店卻取名為「兔屋」，總覺得有點奇怪，據說是因為第一代店主生於卯年才會以兔子為名。仔細看會發現屋頂有可愛的白兔雕像！

紙袋也很可愛！

The paper bag is cute, too!

Lovingly Prepared Dorayaki
With a History of Over 100 Years!

Although the original dorayaki was a single pancake, Usagiya in Tokyo was the first restaurant to create the modern dorayaki made of sweet bean paste sandwiched between two pancakes. The shop has now perfected the use of old and new technologies to create perfect dorayaki every time. The name, Usagiya, means "Rabbit Shop" which may seem odd for a sweets shop. However, the name was chosen because the first generation owner was born in the Chinese year of the rabbit. If you look up to the roof, you can see a little rabbit statue as well!

1.屋頂上的白兔雕像。　2.銅鑼燒單買1個230日圓。　3.1940年左右（左）和1986年左右（右）的店家照片。自創業的1913年以來就一直在這裡營業。　4.氣泡縱向分布在餅皮上，就是吃起來鬆軟的祕訣

1. An iron sculpture of a rabbit on the roof. 2. Dorayaki (230 yen) can be purchased individually. 3. Photos of the shop from 1940 (left) and 1986 (right). The shop has been located here since being founded in 1913. 4. The secret to the fluffy texture is the vertically rising bubbles in the batter.

抹茶巧克力

馬里昂可麗餅 原宿竹下通店
640日圓

法國的可麗餅非常簡樸；餅皮加上奶油、
砂糖、鮮奶油、水果、榛果醬後，用刀叉
切開享用。以街頭小吃來說有點奢華的可
麗餅，誕生於1970年代原宿的「馬里昂
可麗餅」。外層用紙包裝，讓人可以一邊
享受原宿多彩的風景一邊吃可麗餅。

Matcha Chocolate

MARION CRÊPES
Harajuku Takeshita Street Shop
¥640

The French crêpe is delicious and simple, often
topped with things such as butter, sugar, fruit,
or hazelnut sauce. However in the 1970s, the
Harajuku shop "Marion Crepe" created the
Japanese-style eccentric street food crêpe that
is wrapped in a paper cone. The Japanese crêpe
is perfect for this location as you can explore the
colorful neighborhood of Harajuku while eating
this delicious snack.

46 SHOP INFO → P146

47 紅豆麵包
Bean Paste Bun

酒種紅豆麵包

銀座木村家

1個180日圓

「木村屋總本店」是原本為武士的木村安
兵衛，在辭去職務之後所開設的麵包店。
1870年代開業時，麵包才剛開始受大眾
歡迎，為了迎合日本人的口味，所以結合
麵包與紅豆沙推出這項商品，結果馬上爆
紅。至今仍能在銀座的木村家買到紅豆麵
包。

Sakadane Anpan
Ginza Kimuraya
1 Piece ¥180

Kimuraya Sohonten is a bakery founded by
Yasubee Kimura, a former samurai. As bread
was slowly gaining popularity in Japan, he
began experimenting with recipes to make
bread more popular with Japanese people, and
decided to combine sweet bean paste with his
buns. It was an instant hit, and the shop still sells
their famous bean paste buns in Ginza today.

親子丼
Oyakodon

極意 親子丼

玉秀

2800日圓（午餐）

我在美國大學學習日文的時候，教科書上對「親子丼」的解釋非常直接，當時甚至蔚為話題。親子丼的發源店「玉秀」於1760年開業，但初次製作親子丼卻是在大約130年後的1891年。在那之後將近百年的時間都只接受外帶，1970年代開始才能在店內享用。時至今日，大部分的客人仍是為了親子丼造訪。

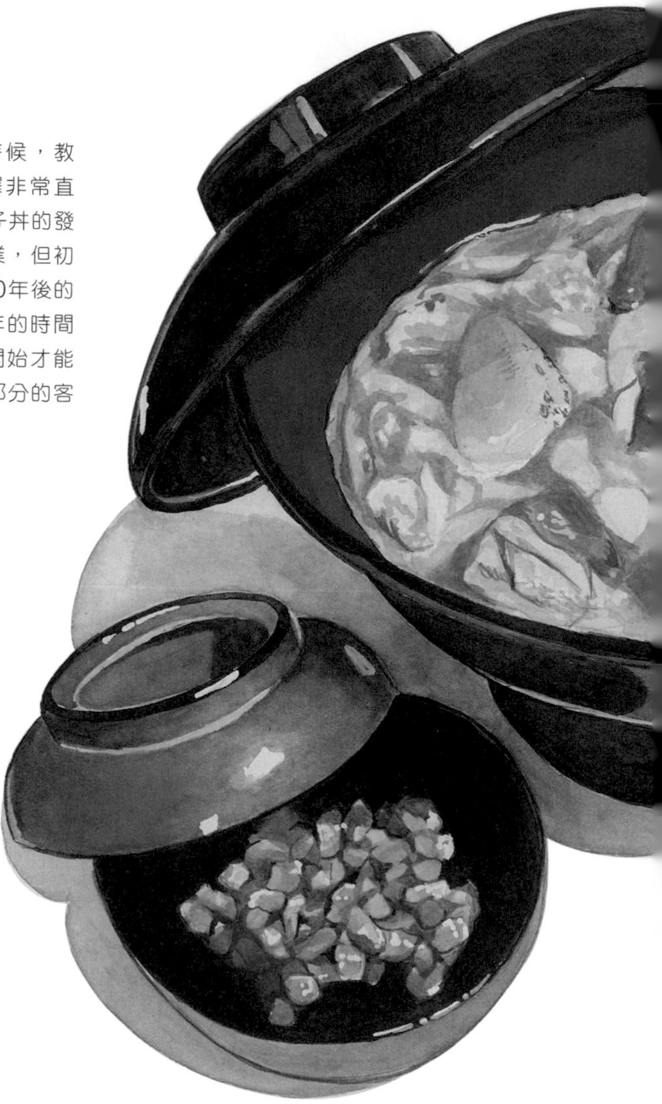

Gokui Oyakodon

Tamahide
¥2800 (Lunch)

When I studied Japanese in America, oyakodon was a dish discussed in our textbook. "Oya" means "parent" and "ko" means "child." The literal trans lation, "parent child rice bowl," repre sents well the the chicken and the eggs served over rice. As new learners of Japanese, we found this quite literal translation amusing. Tamahide restau rant was established in 1760 but didn't develop oyakodon until 1891. For nearly 100 years after that, it was only a dish served by delivery, but in the 1970s they begin providing it within the shop as well. Now a majority of customers come to eat this dish alone.

歐美的麵包不是以三明治的形式吃，就是配菜一起吃，
所以日本的鹹麵包和甜麵包對我來說非常新鮮。
日本的麵包可以直接當作正餐，也可做為零食，
配料、內餡、料理方法非常多樣化。

In America, bread is usually eaten as a sandwich or alongside another
dish as a side element. However, Japan's take on bread is quite
unique. Their sweet and savory breads are a meal or a dessert in
themselves with a large variety of fillings, toppings, and preparations.

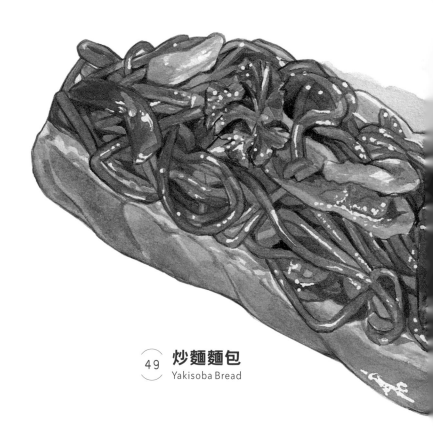

49 **炒麵麵包**
Yakisoba Bread

炒麵麵包

我第一次知道有炒麵麵包這種食物的時候大受衝擊。在國外的確會把義大利麵和麵包放在一起吃，但是我從來沒見過在麵包裡夾炒麵這種食物。麵包類似在美國吃到的熱狗堡，竟然在中間夾入日本的炒麵！雖然很美味，但是碳水化合物加上碳水化合物的組合，我至今仍然覺得很奇怪。

Yakisoba Bread

When I first learned about this dish, I was quite flabbergasted. While pasta and bread wasn't a new concept to me, noodles in bread was. The bread element used here is "koppepan," most similar to a hot dog bun, and it is filled with a popular Japanese street food: yakisoba grilled noodles! Although it's delicious, the carb on carb combination still makes me laugh.

50 菠蘿麵包
Melon Bread

菠蘿麵包
現烤菠蘿麵包 月島久榮
200日圓

我在來日本之前就知道菠蘿麵包，但第一次吃的時候，很驚訝怎麼沒有哈密瓜的味道＊。「菠蘿麵包」這個名稱的由來有兩種說法。最廣為流傳的說法是其酥脆的表皮很像哈密瓜的果皮；另一種說法則是源自「蛋白霜麵包」這個單字。

＊：原文直譯為哈密瓜麵包。

Melon Bread
Freshly Baked Melon Bread - Tsukishima Kyuei
¥200

I had heard of melon bread before coming to Japan but was surprised when I first ate one because... it wasn't melon flavored! There are two theories as to how the name melon bread came about. The more popular theory is that the checkered design on the bread looks like the skin of a musk melon. The second theory is that it was a variation on the word "meringue."

50 SHOP INFO → P147

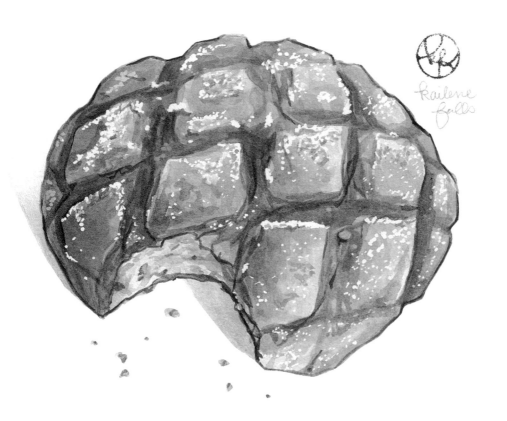

Railene
Balls

NOV.
11 月的散步

—— at ——

月島
Tsukishima

→ ⑤ 菠蘿麵包
Melon Bread

在月島的文字燒街
偶然找到好吃的菠蘿麵包

為了畫插圖，我大多會事前找好店家，但有時候會偶然遇到自己想畫的食物。去月島吃文字燒的時候，找到一間賣菠蘿麵包的小店。這間店就是「現烤菠蘿麵包 月島久榮」。店裡貼滿名人的簽名和電視採訪的照片，一看就知道很受歡迎，當時有買來吃吃看真是太好了！現烤的菠蘿麵包真的很療癒人心呢。外層餅乾的表皮很酥脆，中間則蓬鬆柔軟。

1.櫥窗中飄來現烤菠蘿麵包的甜美香味。　2.也有販售巧克力派和麵包乾等烤餅乾類的商品。　3.月島的西仲通又被稱為「月島文字燒街」，整條街上約有50家文字燒專賣店。

1. The sweet scent of freshly baked melon bread wafts up from the show window. 2. They also sell choco-pies and rusks. 3. The Nishi Nakadori Street in Tsukishima is home to than 50 monjayaki shops.

2.

剛出爐的麵包熱呼呼！
Warm and fresh!

3.

1.

Melon bread that I found by chance on Monja Street in Tsukishima

While I often plan my trips to visit restaurants for food illustrations, sometimes I'm just lucky to stumble across illustration-worthy shops. I had visited Tsukishima to eat monjayaki earlier in the day, and after the meal, I noticed this little stand selling melon bread called "Freshly Baked Melon Bread - Tsukishima Kyuei." Displayed outside of the shop were photos from TV appearances and signatures from celebrities who had visited, indicating it was a popular shop. I definitely didn't regret stopping here! There is something so comforting about freshly baked melon bread. The outside is crunchy and cookie-like, while the inside is soft and moist.

抹茶

2014年當我離開美國時，抹茶在美國終於開始有人氣。
可以在咖啡連鎖店看到抹茶拿鐵，偶爾也會出現抹茶口味的甜點。
然而來到日本之後，抹茶出現的頻率明顯不同。
具有苦澀和濃醇味道的抹茶和各種不同食材搭配，總是讓我很期待。

When I left the US in 2014, matcha was just starting to become a bit
mainstream, with matcha lattes being popular in many chain coffee shops.
However, even now, the variety of matcha treats in America is nowhere
near what you can find in Japan, and I'm always excited to see
new variations with this bitter and complex ingredient.

(51) 抹茶
Matcha

「匠」上生菓子・季節菓子・蜂蜜蛋糕

銀座風月堂
2200日圓

熱水沖開的抹茶直接喝非常苦，我其實
覺得很難入口，而白豆沙也一樣，單吃
會太甜。但是兩者結合之後，苦味和甜
味找到平衡點，變成絕妙美味！坐在這
間店的吧檯座位上，能夠看到師傅製作
白豆沙的樣子，非常有趣。

※ 目前有開放現做和菓子的體驗。

Jo-Namagashi and Tea Set "Takumi"

GINZA FUGETSUDO
¥2200

Traditional matcha is prepared with only
matcha powder and hot water. It is very bitter
and difficult to drink by itself. Therefore, it is
nearly always served alongside some kind of
traditional Japanese sweet. The dessert by
itself is too sweet. The matcha by itself is too
bitter. However together, they balance
beautifully. At this particular shop, I took a
counter seat and was able to watch the
flower-shaped sweet being made by hand in
front of me.

※Currently, you can enjoy watching wagashi being
made with their "Wagashi Making Experience."

MATCHA

51 SHOP INFO → P148

52 抹茶冰淇淋與草糰子
Matcha Ice Cream and Kusa Dango

糰子冰淇淋　紅豆草糰子
日本冰淇淋櫻花

460日圓

我聽說惠比壽有一間店販售把糯米糰子放在冰淇淋上的商品，這讓我非常在意。冰淇淋和糯米糰子可以任意組合搭配，這讓我有點猶豫，不過最後還是決定草糰子、紅豆和抹茶冰淇淋這個組合。在冰淇淋上加糯米糰子我還是第一次吃到，不過味道很搭，溫熱的糰子和冰冷的冰淇淋，兩者的溫度差也是絕妙。

Kusa-An Dango Ice Cream
JAPANESE ICE OUCA

¥460

When I found this shop in Ebisu that features fresh ice cream as a topping for their dango, I was very intrigued. I had a hard time decided which combination of ice cream and dango to buy, but I settled on a kusa (mugwort) dango topped with red beans and matcha ice cream. While the presentation was unusual, the combination of traditional flavors worked perfectly, and the warm dango with cold ice cream was a delicious treat.

52 SHOP INFO → **P148**

抹茶白玉聖代

咖啡茶館 集 Premium 澀谷站前店
1100日圓

抹茶與冰淇淋很搭，所以抹茶聖代也非常
受歡迎。一般來說，會加入白糯米丸、紅
豆沙、栗子等日本風味的配料，和風與西
洋的搭配我覺得恰到好處。另外，這間店
對於聖代中的冰淇淋也很講究，是由店家
親自製作。餘味十分清爽，非常美味。

Matcha Shiratama Parfait

Coffee Sakan SHU Premium
Shibuya Ekimae Shop
¥1100
With matcha pairing so well with ice cream, it
makes perfect sense that matcha parfaits are so
popular in Japan. Usually paired with
ingredients like sweet bean paste, mochi, and
chestnuts, they are a perfect example of
Japanese-style fusion food. This shop makes
their own original ice cream for their parfaits,
and the taste is really light, fresh, and delicious.

抹茶巴巴露亞
Matcha Bavarian Cream

抹茶巴巴露亞
紀之善
961日圓

「巴巴露亞」是歐洲自16～17世紀就有的甜點。混合牛奶、鮮奶油、吉利丁，待凝固之後就完成了。《甘太郎：愛吃甜食的上班族》這部日劇裡面有介紹到提供這款抹茶巴巴露亞、位於神樂坂的店家，之後我就一直想著有一天一定要去吃吃看。帶苦味的抹茶和柔順的巴巴露亞，味道真的是一絕。

Matcha Bavarian Cream
Kinozen
¥961

The dessert called "Bavarian Cream" dates back to 16th or 17th century Europe. It is created by combining milk and whipping cream with some form of gelatin to help it keep its shape. This shop in Kagurazaka is featured in a few different Japanese TV dramas such as "Kantaro: The Sweet Toothed Salaryman," and I wanted to give their famous dessert a try. The richness of the cream plays the perfect counterpart to the bitterness of the matcha.

我在美國明尼亞波利斯市的郊區長大，
雖然當地有咖啡店，但是離家非常遠。
來到東京後發現無論哪一個車站，
周遭都有好幾家咖啡店，這讓我很驚訝。
日本的咖啡店有很多是專賣店，輕鬆的空間裡很適合畫畫。

I grew up in the suburbs of Minneapolis, so while independent cafe's existed, they required a bit of travel to reach. When I came to Tokyo, I was surprised to find so many cafes in every neighborhood I visited. Many Japanese cafes specialize in a certain type of food or drink, and the casual atmosphere creates a chill dining experience. Japanese cafes offer the perfect environment for sketching as well!

55 拉花
Latte Art

客製拉花
帽子咖啡
1200日圓

這幾年，全世界都流行拉花藝術。2D拉花算是基本，最近就連3D拉花也漸漸流行起來。使用打出奶泡的牛奶，像雕刻一樣畫出圖形。這間店可以客製拉花圖案，只要出示自己喜歡的角色或寵物照片，店員就會製作指定圖案的拉花。我請店員用愛貓的樣子設計拉花。

Requestable Latte Art
HATCOFFEE
¥1200

Latte art has been trending around the world for many years. However, while most people are familiar with the 2D art drawn on top of lattes, 3D latte art is slowly gaining in popularity. Using milk foam, the barista carefully builds and sculps the design, and at this latte art specialty cafe, they will do art by request. While many people choose their favorite cartoon character, latte art of pets is also very popular. I showed the barista a photo of my cat, and he made a special drink just for me!

55 SHOP INFO → P150

生火腿・番茄・芝麻菜三明治與小杯拿鐵

CAMELBACK 三明治＆濃縮咖啡

850日圓／550日圓

我在老家吃過各種異國料理，但是來日本之後才第一次吃到「生火腿」。剛開始對這個名稱感到驚訝，擔心吃生的火腿會不會拉肚子，但是口感和味道讓我立刻就愛上。位於奧澀谷的CAMELBACK sandwich&espresso，販售由生火腿、布里起司、萊姆、蜂蜜等高級食材製作的三明治。

Prosciutto, Tomato, and Arugula Sandwich & Small Latte

CAMELBACK sandwich&espresso

¥850／¥550

While I grew up eating a variety of food from a variety of cultures, it wasn't until I came to Japan that I first tried Prosciutto. Called "Raw Ham" in Japanese, the name was a little scary to me at first, but the texture and flavor instantly made me a fan. CAMELBACK sandwich& espresso in Shibuya offers a variety of sandwiches featuring upscale ingredients such as brie cheese, lamb, honey, and of course, "raw ham."

56 SHOP INFO → P150

加州草莓檸檬汽水
甜甜圈
GOOD TOWN 烘焙屋
內用 451 日圓／外帶 442 日圓

剛搬到日本的時候，原本很擔心自己會想
念美國的食物，結果東京的異國料理餐廳
比我想像的還要多。仔細調查後發現，世
界各國的料理專賣店日本幾乎都有。位於
澀谷區的Good Town Bakehouse以現
代美國為概念，是一間從早到晚都能自由
享受餐點的24小時餐廳，這裡的甜甜圈尤
其出色。

California Strawberry
Lemonade Donut
Good Town Bakehouse
EAT IN ¥451 / TO GO ¥442

When I first came to Japan, I was worried about
missing American food. The nice thing about
Tokyo however, is that it offers much multi-
cultural cuisine. If you take the time to do
research, you can find shops featuring foods
from almost any country in the world. This shop
in Shibuya features many classic American
dishes and desserts, and this donut in particular
was such a fun item to paint!

57 **美國甜甜圈**
American Donut

58 期間限定鬆餅
Seasonal Pancake

超級抹茶

阿奎伊咖啡館 惠比壽店

1716日圓（標準尺寸）

在美國，鬆餅是早餐會出現的食物。當然，也有店家會在中餐或晚餐時段提供，但大概是「在中午也能吃到早餐！」的感覺，餐點本身比起日本也樸素很多，因此鬆餅在日本被當成甜點這點我覺得很新鮮！有些店家會將鬆餅佐以豐富的配料，也有店家做得非常厚實，真的就像蛋糕一樣！

※2022年1月的期間限定商品。

Metcha Matcha
cafe accueil Ebisu Shop

¥1716 (Standard Size)

In the US, pancakes are seen as breakfast food. Even when eating them outside of breakfast, they're viewed as a special treat like "breakfast for dinner." I was surprised to come to Japan and see that pancakes are often considered a dessert item. While many have more simple toppings, the decorative and extravagent versions are truly like "cake." Many are made much thicker than US pancakes too, so they well deserve their dessert status.

※This item was available January 2022.

Railene
falls

SHOP INFO

銀座
Ginza

(38) 喫茶 YOU

喫茶 YOU / Cafe YOU

鬆軟滑順的美味蛋包飯最受歡迎！也可以外帶享用。店內有種穿越到昭和時代的氛圍。

📞 03-6226-0482
📍 東京都中央区銀座4-13-17高野ビル1F
🚉 距離地鐵銀座站徒步約1分鐘

Popular for their delicious omurice with a fluffy and soft texture. Takeout is also available. Stepping inside, the shop's design makes you feel like you've travelled back in time to the Showa Era (1926-1989).

📞 +81 3-6226-0482
📍 Takano Building 1F
   4-13-17 Ginza, Chuo-ku, Tokyo
🚉 1-min. walk from the Higashi-Ginza Subway Station

澀谷
Shibuya

(39) Pancho 義大利麵 澀谷店

スパゲッティーのパンチョ 渋谷店 /
Spaghetti no Pancho Shibuya Store

這間拿坡里義大利麵專賣店，持續守護著誕生於日本的飲食文化——「拿坡里義大利麵」。用傳統配方，以講究的料理方法製作而成的拿坡里義大利麵，提供客人懷舊的口味，品牌的口號就是：「希望客人能説出拿坡里義大利麵真好吃這句話」。

📞 03-5489-2522
📍 東京都渋谷区道玄坂2-6-2藤山恒産第一ビルB1F
🚉 距離JR澀谷站徒步約3分鐘

A Napolitan pasta specialty store that works to preserve the "Napolitan" food culture invented in Japan. They are selective in their ingredients and cooking methods, and their pastas have a very nostalgic flavor.

📞 +81 3-5489-2522
📍 Fujiyama Kousan Daiichi Building B1F
   2-6-2 Dogenzaka, Shibuya-ku, Tokyo
🚉 3-min. walk from Shibuya Station

40 炸物亭
ふらい亭 / FryTei

我推薦炸里肌御膳（1540日圓）。使用豬肉最美味的背部，油花恰到好處，非常多汁鮮嫩。

- 📞 03-3411-2989
- 📍 東京都世田谷区野沢2-5-20
- 🚃 距離東急田園都市線駒澤大學站徒步15分鐘

Their "Roast Cutlet Set" (¥1540) comes highly recommended. They use pork loin, which is thought to be the most delicious cut of pork with its juciness and moderate fat content.

- 📞 +81 3-3411-2989
- 📍 2-5-20 Nozawa, Setagaya-ku, Tokyo
- 🚃 5-min. walk from the Komazawa-Daigaku Station on the Tokyu Dentetsu Den-En-Toshi Line

41 義大利麵＆紅酒 壁之穴
パスタ＆ワイン 壁の穴 / Pasta & Wine Kabe no Ana

使用鱈魚子、海膽、納豆等日本食材開發出的義大利麵菜單是該店的經典菜，後來「和風義大利麵」也漸漸風靡全日本。

- 📞 03-3770-8305
- 📍 東京都渋谷区道玄坂2-25-17カスミビル1F
- 🚃 距離各線澀谷站徒步約5分鐘

This shop developed different spaghetti recipes using Japanese ingredients such as cod roe, sea urchin, and natto. These pastas became their specialty, and the concept of "Japanese-style spaghetti," eventually spread from here to the rest of Japan.

- 📞 +81 3-3770-8305
- 📍 Kasumi Building 1F
  2-25-17 Dogenzaka, Shibuya-ku, Tokyo
- 🚃 5-min. walk from Shibuya Station

42 吉野家

吉野家 / Yoshinoya

1899年開業。製作牛丼超過120年。從牛肉、洋蔥、醬汁、白米到生薑皆為嚴選食材,打造出一碗美味的丼飯。

📞 0120-69-5114(客服專線)
◎ 東京都內約有190間分店,日本國內約有1200間分店

Founded in 1899. They have been making beef bowls for over 120 years. A delicious dish with special care paid to the beef, onions, ginger, sauce, and rice used.

📞 +81 120-69-5114 (Customer Support)
◎ About 190 stores in Tokyo / 1,200 stores in Japan

43 CoCo 壹番屋咖哩

カレーハウス CoCo 壱番屋 / CURRY HOUSE CoCoICHIBANYA

不必我多説,這是大家都知道的咖哩專賣店。1號店於1978年在名古屋市郊外開張。之後,不只在日本全國展店,也到亞洲各國、美國等全世界開設分店。

📞 0586-76-7545(總公司)
◎ 東京都內約有170間分店,日本國內約有1240間分店

A well-known curry specialty shop. Their first store opened in 1978 in the suburbs of Nagoya. Since then, they have expanded not only throughout Japan but also to many Asian countries as well as to the USA.

📞 +81 586-76-7545 (Head Office)
◎ About 170 stores in Tokyo / 1,240 stores in Japan

44 麥當勞
マクドナルド / McDonald's

重視每個人的笑容，也重視與家人歡度時光的漢堡店。一般菜單的漢堡很美味，季節限定的品項也不容錯過。

HP https://www.mcdonalds.co.jp
◎ 東京都內約有350間分店，日本國內約有2900間分店

A hamburger shop that provides smiles to both individual customers and familes alike. In addition to their regular burgers, don't miss their variety of seasonal menu items.

HP https://www.mcdonalds.co.jp/
◎ About 350 stores in Tokyo / 2,900 stores in Japan

45 兔屋
うさぎや / USAGIYA

上野
Ueno

大正2年開業。喜作最中餅（120日圓）與銅鑼燒（230日圓）是明星商品。現做的銅鑼燒請務必當場趁熱吃。

☎ 03-3831-6195
◎ 東京都台東区上野1-10-10
🚉 距離JR御徒町站徒步約4分鐘

Founded in 1913. Their signature products are monaka (¥120) and dorayaki (¥230). It is most delicious if you eat the freshly made, warm dorayaki on the spot.

☎ +81 3-3831-6195
◎ 1-10-10 Ueno, Taito-ku, Tokyo
🚉 4-min. walk from the JR Okachimachi Station

(46) 馬里昂可麗餅 原宿竹下通店

マリオンクレープ 原宿竹下通り店 /
MARION CRÊPES Harajuku Takeshita Street Shop

原宿
Harajuku

1976年這間店就開始販售來自法國的可麗餅，之後的40年間，仍持續提供正宗的可麗餅。

📞 03-3401-7297
📍 東京都渋谷区神宮前1-6-15 ジュネスビル1F
🚉 距離JR原宿站徒步約3分鐘

Providing the authentic taste of Japanese crepes for over 40 years. Although crepes originated in France, this was the first shop to sell Japanese style crepes in 1976.

📞 +81 3-3401-7297
📍 JEUNESSE Building 1F
　 1-6-15 Jingumae, Shibuya-ku, Tokyo
🚉 4-min. walk from the JR Harajuku Station

(47) 銀座木村家

銀座木村家 / Ginza Kimuraya

原宿
銀座
Ginza

140多年前，日本首次出現不用酵母，而是用米、酒麴、水發酵後製作出經典的紅豆麵包。法國麵包等西式口味的麵包也很受歡迎。

📞 03-3561-0091
📍 東京都中央区銀座4-5-7 銀座木村家1F
🚉 地鐵銀座站A9出口

Over 140 years ago, this shop was the first shop to make bean paste bread and uses rice, malt, and water instead of yeast to ferment. Their Western-style bread, such as French bread, is also popular.

📞 +81 3-3561-0091
📍 Ginza Kimuraya 1F
　 4-5-7 Ginza, Chuo-ku, Tokyo
🚉 1-min. walk from the A9 Exit of the Ginza Subway Station

48 玉秀
玉ひで / Tamahide

1760年開業的親子丼發源店。在漫長歷史中，受到無數知名人士愛戴的江戶風味，直到現代仍繼續傳承。

📞 03-3668-7651
📍 東京都中央区日本橋人形町1-17-10
🚃 距離地鐵人形町站徒步約1分鐘

This restaurant, established in 1760, was the shop that invented oyakodon. Their classic Edo recipes, loved by many famous historical figures, have been passed down to the present day.

📞 +81 3-3668-7651
📍 1-17-10 Nihonbashi-Ningyocho, Chuo-ku, Tokyo
🚃 1-min. walk from the Ningyocho Subway Station

50 現烤菠蘿麵包 月島久榮
焼き立てメロンパン 月島久栄 /
Freshly Baked Melon Bread - Tsukishima Kyuei

在月島文字燒街邊走邊吃必備的菠蘿麵包。酥脆的菠蘿麵包乾（260日圓～）也很推薦。

📞 03-3534-0298
📍 東京都中央区月島1-21-3
🚃 距離地鐵月島站徒步約3分鐘

This melon bread is perfect for eating while walking on Tsukishima Monja Street. Their crispy melon bread "High Rusks" are also delicious (starting at ¥260).

📞 +81 3-3534-0298
📍 1-21-3 Tsukishima, Chuo-ku, Tokyo
🚃 3-min. walk from the Tsukishima Subway Station

51 銀座風月堂
銀座風月堂 / GINZA FUGETSUDO

輕鬆的和風空間，能夠享受應用四季食材製作的
正宗日本料理與和風甜點。不妨試著透過細緻又
漂亮的甜點，感受季節流轉。

📞 03-3571-2900
📍 東京都中央区銀座6-6-12F
🚇 距離地鐵銀座站B7‧B9徒步約2分鐘

A relaxing Japanese cafe where you can enjoy authentic Japanese food and sweets that use seasonal ingredients. Appreciate the changing of the seasons with delicate and beautiful desserts.

📞 +81 3-3571-2900
📍 2F 6-6-1 Ginza, Chuo-ku, Tokyo
🚇 2-min. walk from the B7 / B9 Exit of the Ginza Subway Station

52 日本冰淇淋櫻花
ジャパニーズアイス櫻花 / JAPANESE ICE OUCA

以當季為主題，從日本各地嚴選食材製作而成的
冰淇淋。請先從可以選擇三種口味的綜合冰淇淋
（450日圓～）開始嘗試。

📞 03-5449-0037
📍 東京都渋谷区恵比寿1-6-7 animo ebisu1F
🚇 距離JR惠比壽站西出口徒步約2分鐘

Ready-to-eat ice cream created with ingredients hand-selected from all over Japan. Begin by choosing three of your favorite flavors with a triple scoop ice cream (starting at ¥450).

📞 +81 3-5449-0037
📍 animo Ebisu1F
   1-6-7 Ebisu, Shibuya-ku, Tokyo
🚇 2-min. walk from the West Exit of the JR Ebisu Station

53 咖啡茶館 集 Premium 澀谷站前店
珈琲茶館 集 プレミアム渋谷駅前店 /
Coffee Sakan SHU Premium Shibuya Ekimae Shop

香氣繚繞、療癒身心的咖啡館。使用全球咖啡產地當季的最高級咖啡豆。可以在大人風格的療癒空間內，度過一段輕鬆時光。

📞 03-3464-9244
📍 東京都渋谷区道玄坂2-29-3 道玄坂共同ビル1F・2F
🚉 距離各線澀谷站徒步約3分鐘

Coffee that heals the body and mind. They select the finest beans harvested in season from coffee-producing regions around the world. Relax and rejuvenate in this classic shop.

📞 +81 3-3464-9244
📍 Dogenzaka Kyodo Building 1F / 2F
2-29-3 Dogenzaka, Shibuya-ku, Tokyo
🚉 3-min. walk from Shibuya Station

54 紀之善
紀の善 / Kinozen

位於神樂坂下區的日式甜點店。除了餡蜜、麻糬紅豆湯、經典的抹茶巴巴露亞等商品之外，四季都有不同的甜點可以選擇。也有提供釜飯等飯類的料理。

📞 03-3269-2920
📍 東京都新宿区神楽坂1-12 紀の善ビル
🚉 距離JR飯田橋站西出口徒步3分鐘

A sweets shop in Kagurazaka, Tokyo. In addition to anmitsu, sweet bean soup, and their classic matcha Bavarian cream, you can enjoy seasonal menu items. They also serve meals like steamed rice dishes.

📞 +81 3-3269-2920
📍 Kinozen Building
1-12 Kagurazaka, Shinjuku-ku, Tokyo
🚉 3-min. walk from the West Exit of the JR Iidabashi Station

（已停業）

SHOP INFO

55 帽子咖啡

ハットコーヒー / HATCOFFEE

活躍於國內外的拉花藝術家 Matsuno Kohei 主理的咖啡店。店內可客製拉花。

📞 03-6874-4750
📍 東京都台東区寿 3-15-6
🚇 距離地鐵田原町站徒步約 4 分鐘

A cafe owned by Matsuno Kohei, a latte artist who is active both in Japan and overseas. You can order custom-made latte art at this shop.

📞 +81 3-6874-4750
📍 3-15-6 Kotobuki, Taito-ku, Tokyo
🚇 4-min. walk from the Tawaramachi Subway Station

56 CAMELBACK 三明治 & 濃縮咖啡

キャメルバック サンドイッチ＆エスプレッソ / CAMELBACK sandwich&espresso

客人點餐後才製作的手工三明治與咖啡。非常適合到奧澀谷與代代木公園散步時享用。

📞 03-6407-0069
📍 東京都渋谷区神山町 42-2
🚇 距離地鐵代代木站徒步約 5 分鐘

A sandwich and coffee shop that handmakes each sandwich upon order. Perfect for a day exploring Oku-Shibuya or Yoyogi Park.

📞 +81 3-6407-0069
📍 42-2 Kamiyamacho, Shibuya-ku, Tokyo
🚇 5-min. walk from the Yoyogi-Koen Subway Station

57 GOOD TOWN 烘焙屋

グッドタウンベイクハウス / Good Town Bakehouse

披薩、啤酒、紅酒與咖啡，充滿美國風格的咖啡店。讓人有種來到國外的感覺，可以在店內度過美妙的時光。

📞 03-6886-5330
📍 東京都渋谷区上原1-30-11F
🚃 距離小田急線代代木上原站徒步約1分鐘

Pizza, beer, wine, and coffee. An American-style cafe. Visit for an international experience.

📞 +81 3-6886-5330
📍 1F 1-30-1 Uehara, Shibuya-ku, Tokyo
🚃 1-min. walk from the Yoyogi Uehara Station on the Odakyu Line

58 阿奎伊咖啡館 惠比壽店

カフェ アクイーユ 恵比寿店 / cafe accueil Ebisu Shop

提供由甜點師製作的鬆餅與咖啡簡餐。除了可愛的甜點與拉花咖啡，特製蛋包飯也很受歡迎。

📞 03-6821-8888
📍 東京都渋谷区恵比寿西2-10-10 エレガンテヴィータ1F
🚃 距離JR惠比壽站・東急東横線代官山站徒步約4分鐘

Pancakes and cafe-style meals made by pastry chefs. In addition to cute sweets and latte art, their special omurice is also popular.

📞 +81 3-6821-8888
📍 Elegante Vita 1F 2-10-10 Ebisu-Nishi, Shibuya-ku, Tokyo
🚃 4-min. walk from the JR Ebisu Station or Daikanyama Station on the Tokyu Toyoko Line.

KYOTO TRIP
with Sketches

KIYOMIZUDERA, KAWARAMACHI, GION, MURASAKINO

My Sketching Tools

鉛筆素描我通常用較硬的鉛筆（2H）畫底稿，然後用較軟的鉛筆（2B）繪製正式的線稿。我很喜歡之前在奈良買的鉛筆延長桿。不知道為什麼用素描本會覺得很有壓力，所以我總是把A5尺寸的水彩紙放在檔案夾裡帶在身邊。

For sketching, I use both a hard lead (2H) and a soft lead (2B) pencil. I'll first draw a very light, rough image before making a darker, finalized image. I also like to use a pen holder that I bought when in Nara. For some reason, using a sketchbook stresses me out. Therefore, I cut paper down to A5 size and bring it in a leather file.

每次去京都，我都能深刻感受到歷史的分量。
京都有很多寺院和商家，都讓人像穿越到過去一樣。
而且還有很多提供美味餐點的店家。我花兩天的時間，帶著素描本，
除了造訪人氣觀光景點，也有探訪一些比較冷門的地方。

When you visit Kyoto, you can really sense the history of the city. From the temples to the shops, you feel like you've traveled back in time. And of course, there is plenty of delicious food as well! I took a two-day trip to Kyoto, visiting a few popular sites as well as some more unusual locations and brought my sketchbook on the way.

清水寺　河原町

旅行的起點就從美麗的京都名勝古蹟開始

Starting the Trip with Some of Kyoto's Most Beautiful and Popular Spots

在清水寺參道散步

我是SOU·SOU的鐵粉。衣櫃裡的衣物和飾品有一半是SOU·SOU的產品。我聽說清水寺參道產寧坂上開了新分店，所以決定去看一看。那附近有地標八坂塔和八坂庚申堂等許多寺院，景觀也很漂亮。散步1個小時左右，就能充分感受京都風味。

Walking the Road to Kiyomizu Temple

I am a huge fan of Sou·Sou. Nearly half of the clothing and accessories in my closet come from this fantastic shop. When I heard that they opened a new location on the famous Sanneizaka Road to Kiyomizu Temple, I knew I had to check it out. The scenery in the area is beautiful, and the symbolic Yasaka Tower and Yasaka-Koshindo Temple nearby are worth a visit too. If you spend about an hour exploring the area, you'll feel like you've had a "Uniquely Kyoto" experience.

產寧坂
Sanneizaka

是連接世界遺產清水寺的參道中的其中一段。石板坡道的兩旁，林立著京都風格的和風建築物。

⊙ 京都府京都市東山区清水2

One of the roads leading to the World Heritage Site "Kiyomizu Temple." Traditional Japanese buildings, typical of Kyoto, line both sides of the cobblestone slope.

⊙ Kiyomizu, Higashiyama-ku, Kyoto-shi, Kyoto

街道本身就非常有趣！
An interesting town!

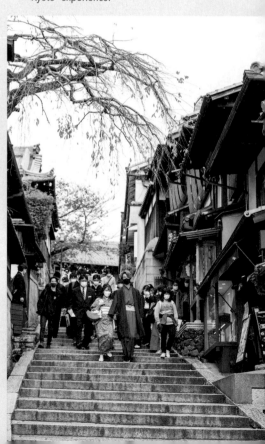

伊藤軒／SOU·SOU
清水店
Itoken Sousou Kiyomizumise

將SOU·SOU的織品設計應用在和菓子老店伊藤軒的商品上。同時販售清水店限定的外帶點心與周邊商品。

📞 0120-929-110
📍 京都府京都市東山区清水3-315

SOU·SOU's popular textile designs have been remade into traditional treats at this old-fashioned Japanese shop. There are many goods and snacks only available at this location.

📞 +81 120-929-110
📍 3-315 Kiyomizu, Higashiyama-ku, Kyoto-shi, Kyoto

上：造型設計甜點串和菓子500日圓。　右：店內也有拍照景點。

Above: Pop-art skewered Japanese sweets, ¥500.
Right: A photo spot within the shop.

⬤ Illustration Notes

SOU·SOU的織品設計中，我最喜歡的就是數字圖案，這款蜂蜜蛋糕就是以數字圖案製作。我想透過插圖呈現漂亮的織品設計，所以買了3種口味排列在擦手巾上。

SO-SU-U羊羹蜂蜜蛋糕（黑糖·10顆裝）1296日圓起

Sou·Sou's unique patterns aren't only for fabric! They used their popular number design for these miniature castella cakes. I bought three different flavors and styled them on a "tenugui" cloth because I really wanted to showcase Sou·Sou's charming textiles too!

SO-SU-U Yokan Caste-Illa
(Brown Sugar, 10 Piece) ¥1296

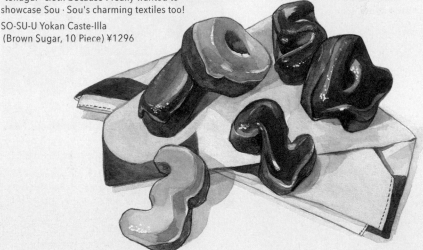

八坂塔
Yasaka No To

建於八坂神社與清水寺中間，通稱「八坂塔」。這座塔其實是法觀寺的五重塔，也是眾所周知的京都地標。

⊙ 京都府京都市東山区八坂上町388

Yasaka Tower is located between Yasaka Shrine and Kiyomizu-Dera. The five-storied pagoda belonging to the Hokanji Temple is also a well-known landmark.

⊙ 388 Yasaka Kamimachi, Higashiyama-ku, Kyoto-shi, Kyoto

旅客來這裡一定會以八坂塔為背景拍攝紀念照。周邊有咖啡店和伴手禮店，很適合休息或散步。

Taking a photo with Yasaka Tower in the background is a must. There are many souvenirs shops and cafes in the area, perfect for browsing or taking a break.

色彩繽紛真可愛！
So cute and colorful!

八坂庚申堂
Yasaka Koshindo

繽紛的祈願吊飾「束猿」非常引人注目。裡面到處都有代表「不看・不言・不聽」的三猿。

☏ 075-541-2565
⊙ 京都府京都市東山区金園町390

The colorful and eye-catching "Kukuri Monkeys." The balls represent monkeys, and the monkeys in turn represent the sentiment "See no evil, hear no evil, speak no evil."

☏ +81 75-541-2565
⊙ 390 Kinencho, Higashiyama-ku, Kyoto-shi, Kyoto

束猿一隻500日圓。據說忍耐一個慾望，就會實現一個願望。

The "Kukuri Monkeys" are ¥500 per piece. Legend says that writing your wish on one will make it come true.

舖滿白砂的波心庭
The white-sanded Hashin Garden.

高臺寺
Kodaiji

這是豐臣秀吉的正室，寧寧為了悼念秀吉而建的寺院。寺內有美麗的庭園，春天有垂枝櫻，秋天則是賞楓的知名景點。

📞 075-561-9966
📍 京都府京都市東山区高台寺下河原町526

A temple built by Toyotomi Hideyoshi's wife Nene to mourn Hideyoshi's passing. The beautiful garden is famous for its weeping cherry blossoms in the spring and fall leaves in autumn.

📞 +81 75-561-9966
📍 526 Kodaiji Shimokawara-cho, Higashiyama-ku, Kyoto-shi, Kyoto

在知名庭園感受秋意

京都的每個季節都很美，不過充滿楓紅的寺院特別讓人感動。美國也有很多楓樹，但樹葉比日本的楓樹大好幾倍，所以我覺得日本的楓紅非常可愛又獨具魅力。我去過京都很多次，但直到這次才終於看到京都的楓紅。

Experiencing Autumn at a Famous Garden

While Kyoto is beautiful to visit any time of year, Kyoto's temples make a particularly beautiful scene when surrounded by fall leaves. Maple trees are common in America too, but their leaves are more than twice as big, so I find Japanese maple trees particularly cute. Although I have visited Kyoto many times in the past, this trip I was finally able to see Kyoto's fall colors.

令人憧憬的七彩果凍潘趣酒

這間懷舊喫茶店是這次旅行我無論如何都想去的地點。在雜誌上看到七彩果凍潘趣酒之後，我不只想把它畫成插圖，還想看看店內漂亮的裝潢。據說這款商品一開始是因為第3代老闆娘小時候討厭喝牛奶，媽媽為了讓女兒對牛奶產生興趣，所以開發出五色果凍牛奶。這道甜品也可以做成潘趣酒或優酪乳等不同的版本，是廣受歡迎超過50年的人氣商品。

The Perfect Jelly Punch

The jelly punch at this retro kissaten was a must-visit for my Kyoto trip. I saw photos of it in a magazine and knew I both wanted to paint it as well as visit the kissaten itself. The granddaughter of the original owner runs this shop and told me that her mother created the five-colored milk version first in order to tempt her into drinking milk. Many variations, including the original milk and other flavors like punch and yogurt, are still sold here over 40 years later.

喫茶 SOWARE
喫茶ソフレ / Kissa Soware

昭和23（1948）年開業的喫茶店。明星商品七彩果凍潘趣酒，以及用裝飾著畫家東鄉青兒畫作的玻璃杯來盛裝的冰淇淋蘇打等，都很受歡迎。

📞 075-221-0351
📍 京都府京都市下京区真町95

A kissaten founded in 1948. The famous jelly punch is popular as well as the cream soda which is served in a glass decorated with an illustration by the painter Seiji Togo.

📞 +81 75-221-0351
📍 95 Shincho, Shimogyo-ku, Kyoto-shi, Kyoto

🔴 Illustration Notes

要漂亮地呈現透明感，重點在於光澤和顏色的層次感。我用清晰的顏色和形狀來呈現潘趣酒，優酪乳則是用稍微不透明的感覺來表達。

七彩果凍潘趣酒750日圓
優酪乳潘趣酒900日圓

To properly convey the transparency of these drinks, I focused on shine and color gradations. With the soda version, the colors and shapes of the gelatin were clearly visible, but they needed to be rendered a bit differently for the yogurt version.

Jelly Punch ¥750
Yogurt Punch ¥900

上：窗外是高瀨川。這裡是有溫柔陽光灑落的貴賓
席。　右：因為想「讓女性看起來更漂亮」，所以照
明都使用鈷藍色。

Above: The Takase River flows outside the
window. It's a wonderful seat where you can enjoy
a bit of sunlight.　Right: The cobalt blue lighting
was designed to "help women look beautiful."

到處都有古董小物以及葡萄的
擺飾，打造出懷舊的空間。

Antique accessories and
grape-themed objects are
displayed about, creating a
retro space.

歡迎來到藍色的世界！
Welcome to
our blue world!

錦市場
Nishiki Ichiba

素有「京都廚房」之稱的市場商店街。
東西長390m的道路上，匯集約120間
餐飲店。

📞 075-211-3882（京都錦市場商店街振
興協會）
📍 京都府京都市中京区西大文字町609

A shopping street referred to as
"Kyoto's Kitchen." Approximately
120 food-related shops line the
390m street running east to west.

📞 +81 75-211-3882
📍 609 Nishidaimonji-cho, Nakagyo-
ku, Kyoto-shi, Kyoto

我吃了鱸魚天婦羅！
I ate some conger eel tempura!

到市場尋找京野菜

日本有很多美味的蔬菜，但是京都的蔬菜有名
到擁有「京野菜」這個專有名詞。其中有很多
富含高營養價值、外觀造型獨特的蔬菜。錦市
場有很多街頭小吃（不能邊走邊吃）和紀念品
店，當然也有京野菜的專賣店。我在市場稍
微吃過一點東西之後，就前往販售京野菜的店
家。

Heading to the Market to Find Some Kyo-Yasai

While there are many delicious vegetables found
all across Japan, Kyoto's heirloom vegetables are
famous enough to have their own label: "Kyo-Yasai".
They are knkown for being particularly nutrient rich,
and they come in a variety of unique sizes and shapes.
Nishiki Market is filled with shops selling street foods
(walking while eating is banned), souvenirs, and of
course, even a Kyo-Yasai shop. After snacking a bit in
the market, I made my way to the Kyo-Yasai shop and
took the opportunity to peruse their selection.

● Illustration Notes

這間店陳列蔬菜的方式非常有魅力，有很多我沒見過的蔬菜。難得來一趟，我並不想只畫一種蔬菜，而是想要描繪充滿市場感的蔬菜陳列架一隅。手寫的價格牌POP很有感覺！

The rows of vegetables at this shop were really charming, and a few of the varieties I didn't even recognize. I decided to sketch a section of the shop display that really conveyed the "market" feel. Handwritten signs add an extra element of authenticity!

上：葉子嫩綠水潤的京都水菜，從外觀就可以感受到蔬菜的新鮮度。　下：我手上拿的大蘿蔔是「聖護院白蘿蔔」，這是傳統的京野菜之一。

Top: Mizuna greens with lush leaves. You can just feel their freshness by looking at them. Bottom: The big radish is called a "Shogoin Radish." It is a traditional variety of "Kyo-Yasai."

四寅
Yontora

明治43（1910）年開業的老牌蔬果店。以京野菜為主，嚴選當季最美味的高品質蔬菜與水果。

📞 075-221-2730
📍 京都府京都市中京区鍛冶屋町221

An historical fruit and vegetable store founded in 1910. They sell only the most delicious and high quality vegetables and fruit available, focusing on "Kyo-Yasai."

📞 +81 75-221-2730
📍 221 Kajiya-machi, Nakagyo-ku, Kyoto-shi, Kyoto

御旅宿 月屋
Bed&Breakfast Tsukiya

能夠充分感受京町屋風情的旅店
（B&B、附早餐）。有4個以月亮為主
題的房間。每人1晚7000日圓～。

📞 075-353-7920
📍 京都府京都市下京区蛭子町139-1

Lodgings (breakfast included) where
you can fully feel the atmosphere of
a traditional Kyoto house. There are
four private rooms, each named after
the moon. From ¥7000 per person
per night.

📞 +81 75-353-7920
📍 139-1 Ebisu-cho, Shimogyo-ku,
Kyoto-shi, Kyoto

住在京町屋

京都有很多好飯店，但是我比較喜歡住在老式
的京町屋。從老舊木材打造的外觀到擺設古董
傢俱的裝潢，「月屋」都是最具代表的京町
屋。這裡的和服攝影體驗也很受歡迎！是能透
過自製早餐感受京都文化的美好旅宿。

Staying at a Kyoto Townhouse

While there are many nice hotels in Kyoto, I prefer
staying in traditional Kyoto townhouses. From
its wooden exterior to its interior with antique
furnishings, Tsukiya is a wonderful representation
of a classic Kyoto house. It's a popular location to
rent for classic Japanese photoshoots as well! The
addition of the homemade breakfast was the perfect
way to get the whole Kyoto-experience.

● Illustration Notes

這種風格的浴缸很罕見又可愛，
但是拍照的時候視角不夠寬廣，
只好用插畫表現了！雖然寬度很
窄，但是比國外的浴缸還深，可
以浸泡到肩膀。

I found the bath area
particularly charming, but
the angle of the washroom
made it difficult to get
a good picture... so I
decided to illustrate it!
Despite having a small
footprint, the depth of
the bathtub means that
you can still submerge to
your shoulders.

換穿浴衣！
Wear a yukata robe!

我入住的房間是2樓的「望月」。6張榻榻
米的房間裡有一個大壁龕，還連接一個4張
榻榻米的房間，是間非常寬敞的和室。古老
的裝潢和浴衣，都能讓人感受到古典的日本
文化。

A stay in the room "Mochizuki" on the 2nd floor. The spacious
Japanese-style lodgings include a four-tatami mat room and a
six-mat room with a large alcove. You can appreciate old Japanese
culture through the vintage interior and provided yukata robe.

追尋新舊融合
層次更深的京都

Old and New: Exploring Kyoto Deeper

早晨的祇園散步

祇園是京都很熱門的攝影地點，所以避開人潮擁擠的時間，一大早去才能拍到最漂亮的照片，有時候即便是一大早去還是需要排隊等待。我造訪京都的時候，有很多新婚夫妻在拍攝婚紗。石板路、紅色圍牆、古老的燈籠還有可愛的小橋，成為熱門景點也是理所當然的事情！

An Early Morning Walk in Gion

This spot in Kyoto is particularly popular for pictures, so to avoid the crowds, it's best to arrive early in the morning. Nevertheless you still may need to wait your turn! When I visited, there were multiple couples taking wedding pictures at this site, and it's no wonder. The cobblestone, the red fences, the traditional lanterns, and the bridge all make for a really photogenic location.

祇園白川
Gion Shirakawa

白川沿岸可以看到成排的櫻花樹和柳樹，是個可以享受四季不同風情的地方。巽橋附近是絕佳的攝影地點。

⊙ 京都府京都市東山区清本町372

The Shirakawa River is lined with rows of cherry blossom trees and willow trees, so you can enjoy different scenery each season. This spot near Tatsumi Bridge is great for photos.

⊙ 372 Kiyomoto-cho, Higashiyama-ku, Kyoto-shi, Kyoto

早晨的陽光讓人心情舒暢！
A lovely morning!

花見小路
Hanami Koji

這條街上都是老字號的茶屋和高級料理亭，是通往祇園中心的主要道路。運氣好的話，或許能遇見藝伎或舞伎喔。

◎ 京都府京都市東山区祇園町南側

The main street that runs through the center of Gion, lined with long-established teahouses and restaurants. If you are lucky, you may see Geiko (Geisha) and Maiko.

◎ South side of Gion-Machi, Higashiyama-ku, Kyoto-shi, Kyoto

● Illustration Notes

我非常喜歡舞伎們身上的傳統服飾打扮。在花見小路上遇到她們時就決定畫下來！漂亮的日本髮髻、羽織外套令人心生嚮往。

I love the traditional fashion of Maiko, so I decided to illustrate these Maiko that I saw on the Hanamikoji road. Their elegant hair and beautifully patterned kimonos and coats really were lovely.

左：花見小路是一條綿延1km左右的石板路。
右上：宛如電影畫面的街道。
右下：發現屋頂上有除魔大神鍾馗。

Left: Hanamikoji is a cobblestone street that stretches for about 1 km. Upper right: A photogenic town scene, almost like a movie set. Lower right: Spotting a Shoki Talisman on the roof.

前身是錢湯的咖啡店

客人減少之後很多行業都消失了，不過這棟前身為錢湯的建築物以別的形式重生……變成咖啡店！利用懷舊的氛圍，保留原本錢湯的磁磚，打造成一個時尚的空間。很適合用餐、喝下午茶、稍事休息。

Renovated Bathhouse Cafe

When customers grow few, most businesses are forced to close. However, this traditional bathhouse found another way to survive... as a cafe! The bones of the sento remain: the original layout, old wood, and tiles. However, it now functions as a unique and stylish place to have a meal or tea.

熱騰騰！鐵板巧克力布朗尼～搭配冰淇淋～750日圓、飲料550日圓

Super hot! A chocolate brownie with ice cream served on an iron plate for ¥750 and drink ¥550.

更紗西陣

さらさ西陣 / Sarasa Nishijin

由昭和的澡堂建築改造而成的咖啡店。
店內的牆壁、廁所、挑高的天花板等，
隨處都可以感受到錢湯的風格。

📞 075-432-5075
📍 京都府京都市北区紫野東藤ノ森町11-1

A Showa Era public bath renovated into
a cafe. Remnants of the public bath are
everywhere, including the walls, the
restrooms, and the atrium ceiling.

📞 +81 75-432-5075
📍 11-1 Murasakino, Higashi-
   Fujinomori-cho, Kita-ku, Kyoto-
   shi, Kyoto

上：牆上的磁磚是從錢湯時
代就留下來的。　右：這是
以前置物櫃的門板。

Above: The tiles on the wall
remain as they were when
it was a public bath. Right:
A former locker door.

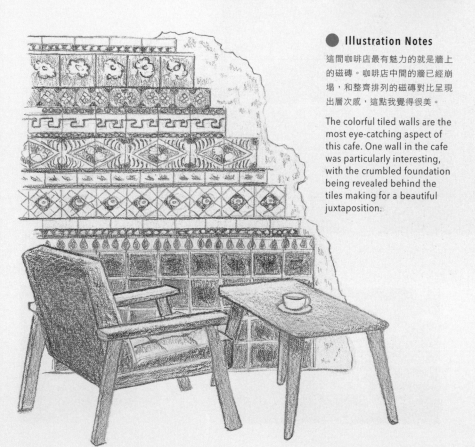

● Illustration Notes

這間咖啡店最有魅力的就是牆上
的磁磚。咖啡店中間的牆已經崩
塌，和整齊排列的磁磚對比呈現
出層次感，這點我覺得很美。

The colorful tiled walls are the
most eye-catching aspect of
this cafe. One wall in the cafe
was particularly interesting,
with the crumbled foundation
being revealed behind the
tiles making for a beautiful
juxtaposition.

167

找尋日本的古董

紀念品店雖然也很好，但是要買給自己的紀念品，我比較喜歡到當地的古董店選購。購物本身就已經開心，把從前當地人愛惜的物品帶回家，我覺得很有趣也是很棒的回憶。日本有很多蒐集歐美古董的店家，但是這裡專營日本古董，最適合找尋京都的寶物了！

Hunting for Japanese Antiques

Standard souvenir shops are nice, but when buying a souvenir for myself, I like to visit local antique shops. Looking through the items is fun, and bringing home something that was loved by a local decades ago is much more interesting and memorable for me. Many antique shops in Japan specialize in antiques from Europe or America, but this shop in Kyoto specialized in Japan-specific items, making it the perfect spot to go treasure hunting.

上：硯臺盒1萬7500日圓。這是一種可以同時攜帶毛筆與硯臺的文具。　右：紅鶴圖案的多層盒8萬4000日圓。

Above: A "Yatate" for ¥17500. Used to carry brushes and ink.
Right: A set of food boxes with a crane design for ¥84000.

● Illustration Notes

在舖有榻榻米的房間裡擺放一盞這種燈，就能感受到令人懷念的昭和時代。我特別喜歡這種混合現代和風的感覺。

When this type of lamp decorates a tatami room, you really feel transported back to the Showa Era. I really like this period of mixing Western and Eastern aesthetics.

古董專家 古夢
**プロアンティーク 古夢 /
Pro Antiques COM**

專門蒐集京都古董的古董專賣店。希望顧客能在感受老工具背後的歷史氛圍之餘，也把這些舊物融入生活中，所以提供修復出售商品的服務。

📞 075-254-7536
📍 京都府京都市中京区東片町616

An antique shop specializing in antiques from all over Kyoto. They also repair the items so that you can both feel the history of old objects and incorporate them into your own life.

📞 +81 75-254-7536
📍 616 Higashi-Katamachi, Nakagyo-ku, Kyoto-shi, Kyoto

色彩繽紛的手織壽司

AWOMB是一間擁有嶄新概念的餐廳。使用當季食材，提供蔬食手織壽司。食材不僅限於蔬菜，也會結合水果、辛香料等特殊的配料。這樣的概念非常適合喜歡嘗鮮的我。嘗試從未想過的搭配組合非常有趣而且美味！

Colorful 'Hand Woven' Sushi

AWOMB is a sushi shop with a very interesting concept. Using seasonal and local ingredients, AWOMB offers "weave-it-yourself" vegetarian sushi. The ingredients change regularly and incude fruit, vegetables, and seasonings that can be used in a variety of unique combinations. I'm always open to trying something new, and this delicious and fun experience definitely didn't disappoint!

AWOMB 西木屋町
アウーム 西木屋町 /
AWOMB Nishikiya-Machi

「手織壽司」提供約50種食材配料，讓客人自行做成手捲。完全不使用動物性蛋白質，非常健康。

📞 050-3177-5277
📍 京都府京都市下京区難波町405

Offering "hand-woven" sushi that you can create by hand-rolling roughly 50 different ingredients. No animal proteins are used, making for a healthy meal.

📞 +81 50-3177-5277
📍 405 Namba-Cho, Shimogyo-ku, Kyoto-shi, Kyoto

● Illustration Notes

因為畫面裡有太多素材，所以我一度猶豫要不要只畫大盤子裡面的配料就好。但是又覺得沒畫海苔和調味料就無法傳達出其獨特的魅力，最後還是全部都畫出來了！

手織壽司 3267 日圓

Because there were so many parts to this dish, I was tempted to illustrate only the main plate. However, the concept couldn't be conveyed without the nori seaweed, rice, and seasonings, so I ended up painting the whole thing!

Teori-Sushi YOH ¥3267

左：改造老舊京町屋，打造出典雅的空間。
右：要用海苔包哪些食材、從餐盤上的哪一樣開始包都OK。用你自己的方式搭配，吃吃看吧！

Left: A stylish space renovated from an old Kyoto townhouse. Right: You can choose any of the plated ingredients to wrap with the nori seaweed. Make your own original combinations.

12　1　2　3
月　月　月　月

WINTER

December

January

February

March

冬天有聖誕節又有新年，節慶特別多。
當然，這種日子一定會伴隨很多美食！
在寒冷的日子享受溫暖的料理，是至高無上的幸福！

Hosting both Christmas and New Years, winter is filled with lots of celebrations.
Of course, many delicious foods accompany these festivities as well!
What's better than eating a warm meal on a cold day?

壽司

我小時候曾經被魚刺哽住喉嚨，所以只要是魚我都不喜歡。
然而，我開始學日文的時候，得知日本飲食中有很多魚類料理，
就想著一定要變得能吃魚才行。因此，我從完全沒有魚骨的「壽司」
開始嘗試，托壽司的福我才變得喜歡吃魚。

When I was young, getting a fishbone caught in my throat resulted in me
hating all fish. When I started studying Japanese though, I realized that
fish was a staple of Japanese cuisine and wanted to learn to like it.
The first fish I was able to eat was sushi since I could get used to the flavor
without fearing bones. Thanks to sushi, I now like fish!

59 江戶前壽司
Edo-Mae Sushi

3代目十二貫
築地青空三代目
4950日圓

Sandaime's Twelve Piece Sushi
Tsukiji Aozora Sandaime
¥4950

原本超討厭吃魚的我後來變得愛吃魚了，這讓我了解到這個世界上沒有讓人討厭一輩子的食物，一切都是托壽司的福。壽司菜單裡我最喜歡無菜單套餐。剛開始會覺得全部都交給壽司師傅決定有點抗拒，但是當食材品質都很優良的時候，我知道只要交給專業的壽司師傅，就能吃到一頓美味的餐點。

After seafood-hate changed to seafood-love, I realized that there wasn't anything I couldn't learn to like. Thanks to sushi, I learned how to enjoy any food, and now I always get excited at "omakase" courses. The idea of leaving all the choices to the chef is intimidating, but when you know the quality is good, you can completely trust the sushi chef to prepare a delicious selection for you.

SUSHI

59 SHOP INFO → P210

1.

DEC.
12 月的推薦

———— at ————

築地青空三代目
Tsukiji Aozora Sandaime

———————

→ 59 江戶前壽司
Edo-Mae Sushi

**如果想在吧檯座享用無菜單壽司
一定要來這裡！**

無菜單套餐很多都是難以負擔的高價品項，但是在築地青空三代目可以吃到品質優良、對錢包友善的江戶前壽司。三代目的石川太信先生的祖父當年來到築地擺攤賣魚，所以從小就在築地長大。築地青空三代目基本上都在吧檯座提供江戶前壽司。因為可以看到壽司師傅捏壽司的過程，所以我最喜歡採用吧檯座的壽司店。

1.吧檯後的松樹是以能劇舞臺為主題的繪畫。　2.在傳統的江戶前壽司中加入現代元素是這間店的特色。醋飯使用米醋等4種不同的醋調和。　3.看著壽司師傅迅速捏好壽司並且漂亮擺盤，就像在看一場秀一樣。

59 SHOP INFO → **P210**

2.

Try This Restaurant for an Omakase-Course Dining Experience with Counter Seating!

Many omakase courses are prohibitively expensive, but at Tsukiji Aozora Sandaime, you can eat Edo-Mae style sushi at a very reasonable price. The third generation owner, Motonobu Ishikawa grew up in the fish market because his grandfather was a fish monger in Tsukiji. The shop adheres to the Edo sushi tradition and provides counter-style sushi. I love counter style sushi since you can see the chefs as they skillfully cut and assemble a variety of different sushi in front of you.

1. The art of the pine tree on the wall is a motif inspired by Noh Theatre. 2. Combining modern ideas with traditional Edo-Mae sushi. The sushi vinegar is made with a blend of four types of vinegar including rice vinegar. 3. A meal with a show featuring the chef preparing beautiful sushi at a remarkable speed.

3.

60 迴轉壽司
Conveyor Belt Sushi

握壽司與軍艦壽司

魚米 澀谷道玄坂店
110日圓～

日本是國際公認擅長應用尖端科技的國
家，迴轉壽司特別讓人有這種感覺。位於
澀谷的魚米是一間走現代摩登風格的店，
用平板等工具點餐，高速軌道就會把餐點
一一送到餐桌上。因為設計實在太新穎，
所以只要有朋友從國外遠道而來，我一定
會帶他們去吃。

Nigiri Sushi and Gunkan

Uobei Shibuya Dougenzaka Store
From ¥110

Japan is internationally thought of as a high-
tech country. One area you can see this is with
conveyor belt sushi. Modern shops like Uobei
in Shibuya use digital tablets to order your item
which is then delivered plate by plate on a
conveyor belt directly to your table. It's such a
novelty that I always bring my foreign friends
for convey or belt sushi when they visit Japan.

60 SHOP INFO → P210

61 散壽司
Bara-Chirashi

散絲壽司
銀座帆掛
6000日圓～

散壽司的名稱來自動詞「散開」，是一種把壽司配料切碎撒在醋飯上的料理。絲壽司則是用非生食的食材取代生魚片。外觀色彩豐富，經常在女兒節等節慶時享用。

Bara-Chirashi
Ginza Hokake
From ¥6000

"Chirashi" comes from the Japanese word "scatter" and is a dish made of a variety of scattered sushi ingredients over a bowl or box of sushi rice. Bara-chirashi is a variation that uses cooked or prepared ingredients rather than raw ingredients. Colorful and delicious, chirashi sushi is often eaten at celebrations such as Girl's Day in March.

62 稻荷壽司
Inari Sushi

福壽家的伊奈利卷
福壽家
1組6個980日圓

稻荷壽司這個名稱的由來，是因為稻荷神的使者狐狸最喜歡吃豆皮，才會取名為稻荷。在甜甜的豆皮中塞入醋飯，是非常簡樸的一道料理，即便是吃素的人也能享用。這間店的稻荷壽司更加高級，還加入了新鮮又多彩的蔬菜。

Fukujuya's Inari Roll
Fukujuya
6 Piece Set ¥980

Inari sushi gets its name from the inari diety's fox-spirit familiars called "inari" who are said to like fried tofu skins. The most common version is made simply of sushi rice wrapped in sweetened tofu skins, and it is a good option for vegetarians. This shop made a fancier version of inari sushi by adding colorful, fresh veggies as filling.

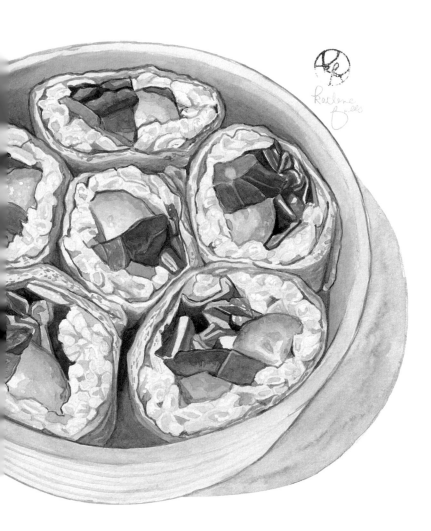

在歐美，除了巧克力之外很少把食物當成禮物。
我真的很喜歡禮品和紀念品。送禮當然希望對方能感受到心意，
不過對方並沒有一直保存禮物的義務啊。
在日本的觀光景點一定會販售紀念品，不僅種類繁多，
其中不乏有趣又漂亮的東西。

Aside from chocolate, the US doesn't have a tradition of giving food as gifts.
I love the concept of omiyage (souvenirs) and temiyage (house-visiting gifts),
as they show care and appreciation for the recipient without obligating them
to keep permanent items.
Since all tourist spots in Japan sell these items,
you can always find something new, unique, and beautiful.

63 手工牛奶糖
Handmade Caramel

8PCS BOX
數字牛奶糖 表參道店
918日圓

朋友從韓國來日本旅行時我才知道這間
店，聽說在韓國很流行拿這家牛奶糖作
為伴手禮。不只有鹽味生薑、覆盆子等
有趣的口味，就連包裝也很美。如果抓
好時間點，還能在店裡看到牛奶糖的製
作過程。

8PCS BOX
NUMBER SUGAR Omotesando Shop
¥918

I first learned about this shop when a
friend visiting from Korea told me about it.
Apparently, in Korea, these caramels are a
popular souvenir to bring back for friends.
There are variety of interesting flavors like
ginger, salt, and raspberry all with beautiful
packaging. Plus, if you time it right, you can
watch the staff make the caramels right in
front of you.

64 金平糖
Sugar Candies

金平糖「彩虹星星」系列
銀座 綠壽庵清水
各1080日圓

金平糖是1546年葡萄牙傳教士送給
織田信長的禮物。雖然受到好評，但
由於原料使用白砂糖，在當時是非常
高價的商品。乍看之下雖然簡樸，但
以新引粉為中心讓砂糖產生結晶，整
個過程大約需要耗費兩週的時間。金
平糖專賣店「銀座 綠壽庵清水」的金
平糖味道非常紮實，從食材和外形都
能感受到店家的用心。最適合當作漂
漂亮亮的伴手禮。

Konpeito "Rainbow Star" Series
Ginza Ryokujuan Shimizu
¥1080 Per Pack

Sugar candies were first introduced to
Japan in 1569 as a gift from Portugal to
Nobunaga Oda, an important historical
figure. They were very expensive as they
used the then rare ingredient: sugar. While
seemingly a simple treat, the process of
turning rice flour and sugar into candies
takes two weeks to complete. The Konpeito
at Ryokujuan have distinct flavors and a
variety of interesting shapes – perfect for
a souvenir.

王林蘋果
1050日圓

Orin Apple
¥1050

甘王草莓
1050日圓

Amaou Strawberry
¥1050

柚子
1050日圓

Yuzu
¥1050

礦物和菓子

harapecolab

4顆裝1000日圓～

乍看之下很像寶石，但是其實是用寒天和
砂糖製成的和菓子。商品名稱是琥珀糖。
待糖凝固之後，切割成礦物或寶石的形
狀。隨時間經過，外層會結晶化，變成脆
硬的糖果，能夠感受到香檳或薄荷等優雅
的香氣。

Koubutsu Wokashi

harapecolab

4 Piece Set from ¥1000～

At first glance, these may look like rock crystals,
but in actuality, they are wagashi (Japanese
confections) called "kohakuto," made from
agar-agar and sugar. Cut into crystalline shapes
and coated with a thin and crisp sugary coating,
subtle flavors like mint and champagne make
these a really fancy treat.

65 SHOP INFO → P213

水果三明治 花田／葡萄花

INITIAL中目黑
1080日圓／843日圓

以外國人的眼光來看，水果三明治是非常奇怪的食物。不過，日本的吐司比外國的白吐司更香甜鬆軟，所以加上鮮奶油和水果就會變成美味的甜點。最近在「INITIAL中目黑」這種時尚的餐廳，很流行利用水果剖面設計出花朵樣式的三明治。

Fruit Sandwiches: Flower Field/ Red Grape Flower

INITIAL Nakameguro
¥1080 / ¥843

From a non-Japanese perspective, fruit in sandwiches is weird. However, Japanese "shokupan" is fluffier and sweeter than most other white breads, and when paired with cream and fruit, it turns into a delicious dessert. Recently, shops such as Initial in Nakameguro have even created sandwiches that look like floral designs, using the sliced fruit in artistic ways.

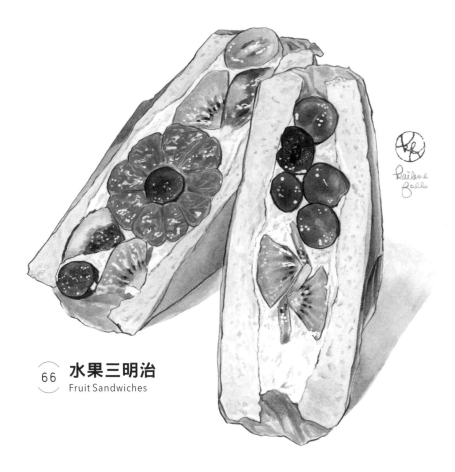

66 水果三明治
Fruit Sandwiches

日本的節慶食物大多是固定的。
雖然全世界四季分明的國家很多，但是日本有很多特定的節慶食物和活動，讓人更容易感受季節的流轉。
這裡要介紹的是冬季節慶會吃的食物。

Japan has a large variety of foods that are specific to special events or times of year. While many other countries can also claim to have "four seasons," Japan's unique seasonal activities and food allow people to really enjoy each season to the fullest. This section will focus on food eaten during the winter months.

FOOD FOR	聖誕節 Christmas

67 草莓奶油蛋糕
Strawberry Shortcake

奶油蛋糕 (白奶油)
法國英鎊屋
713日圓

在日本，草莓奶油蛋糕是生日等節日必吃的經典甜點，最有趣的是聖誕節也會吃。在美國，聖誕節的甜點只有餅乾，所以我第一次在聖誕節的時候吃蛋糕就是在日本。草莓季明明是4～6月，但日本為了配合聖誕節的時間，會使用溫室種植草莓。像FRENCH POUND HOUSE這樣的店家，甚至連搭配蛋糕的草莓品種都很講究。

Shortcake (Blanc)
FRENCH POUND HOUSE
¥713

Strawberry shortcake is the most popular dessert for birthdays and celebrations in Japan. Interestingly, it is also eaten at Christmastime. In America, the standard Christmas dessert is the Christmas cookie, so the first time I ate Christmas cake was in Japan. Despite strawberries being in season from April to June, Japan has perfected greenhouse growing and other techniques to produce enough strawberries for the Christmas season. Shops such as the FRENCH POUND HOUSE select the variety of strawberries that best matches their shortcake recipe.

EVENT FOODS

67 SHOP INFO → P214

68 年菜料理
Osechi

年菜文化非常有趣。從元旦前1～2天就開始準備，每道料理都富含新年新希望，具有獨特的意義。因為事前準備好大量的料理，新年就可以全家人一起悠閒度過。為了能夠久放，很多料理都會加入大量的砂糖和食鹽。

※插圖為作者自行料理。

The Osechi New Year's Box is a tradition that I have always found very interesting. Generally prepared a day or two before New Years, each part of the box has a special meaning or wish for the coming year. By preparing it in advance, people are able to rest the first few days of the New Year and eat this food instead of cooking. A lot of sugar and salt is used in preparation to preserve the ingredients.

※The subject of this illustration was hand-prepared by the author.

年菜每種食材的意義

1　伊達卷 - 增添智慧
2　蓮藕 - 預見未來
3　醋醃牛蒡 - 祈求開運
4　黑豆 - 祈求勤勉與健康
5　紅白魚板 - 紅色除魔、白色表示潔淨
6　醋醃紅白蘿蔔 - 祈求和平與平安
7　蝦子 - 祈求長生
8　昆布卷 - 祈求開啟智慧
9　炒小魚乾 - 祈求豐收
10　鯡魚卵 - 祈求懷孕或子孫滿堂
11　栗子金團 - 祈求好運

Meaning of Osechi Ingredients

1. Rolled Egg - Increased Knowledge
2. Lotus Root - Clear View of the Future
3. Burdock Root - Good Luck
4. Black Beans - Diligence and Health
5. Red & White Fish Cakes - Red to Ward off Evil, White to Purify
6. Red & White Pickles - Peace
7. Shrimp - Long Life
8. Rolled Seaweed - Increased Knowledge
9. Sardines - Fertility
10. Herring Roe - Prosperity for Children and Descendants
11. Chestnuts - Luck in Wealth

69 年糕湯
Ozoni

據說年糕湯是源自於獻給神明的供品。全日本都吃得到年糕湯，但各地的年糕形狀、味噌、高湯、蔬菜、堅果等食材和料理方式都不同。這次畫的年糕湯是關東口味，但我想每年都吃吃看不同的口味！

※插圖為作者自行料理。

Ozoni is a soup eaten at New Years. The tradition was begun as people ate the leftover soup originally offered to the gods. Each area of Japan has its own traditional toppings and preparation - square mochi, round mochi, clear broth, miso soup, vegetables, nuts, etc. The ozoni pictured here is Kanto style, but I would love to try a different variety every year!

※The subject of this illustration was hand-prepared by the author.

70 紅豆年糕湯
Oshiruko

小倉紅豆年糕湯（冬季）
虎屋 赤坂店
1袋627日圓

很多人會在新年吃紅豆年糕湯。鳥取縣會把紅豆年糕湯當作年菜的年糕湯來吃。亞洲有很多國家都喜歡甜湯，但在歐美甜湯很罕見。在和菓子店「虎屋」購買的紅豆年糕湯組合非常豪華，不過日本的自動販賣機也有販售便宜的紅豆年糕湯，讓我很驚奇。

Ogura Shiruko(winter)
Toraya Akasaka Shop
¥627 Per Pack

Sweet bean paste soup with mochi is a popular treat in the winter, especially at New Years. In Tottori prefecture, it is even eaten in place of ozoni soup. Sweet soups are popular in Asia, but are much less common in the Western world. Pictured here is a high qualty shiruko set from the famous Japanese confectionery store Toraya, but you can even find cheap versions of shiruko in vending machines.

71 **惠方卷**
Ehomaki

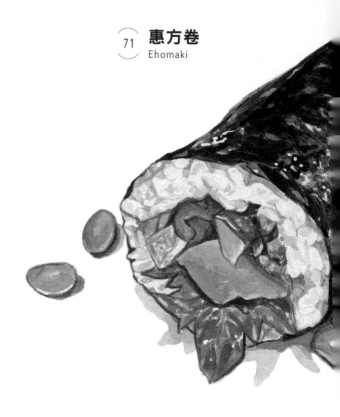

節分是每年2月3日前後的日本節慶。
這一天人們會對戴著鬼怪面具的人喊：
「鬼在外！福在內！」然後邊喊邊撒黃
豆來驅除邪氣。

Setsubun is a holiday that falls around March
3rd. On this day, there is a tradition of casting
away evil spirits by throwing soybeans at
people wearing ogre masks.

在節分這天吃惠方卷原本是關西地區的習俗，但是後來擴散到全日本，近年來日本人都會在節分這天吃惠方卷。據說朝著惠方（吉位）默默吃下惠方卷就能獲得幸運。吉位每年都不一樣，這個習俗非常受歡迎，甚至連新聞都會公布今年的吉位在哪裡。原本惠方卷裡面只有包壽司的配料，現在也經常看到包肉或炸物的惠方卷。

※ 插圖為作者自行料理。

The tradition of eating ehomaki at Sctsubun originated in Kansai, but has spread throughout all of Japan in recent years. You are supposed to eat a whole ehomaki in silence while standing and facing the lucky direction. Each year the direction is different, but it's so popular you can see the direction announced on the TV news. Traditionally ehomaki was made with sushi ingredients, but nowdays you can find them with meats and fried ingredients as well.

※The subject of this illustration was hand-prepared by the author.

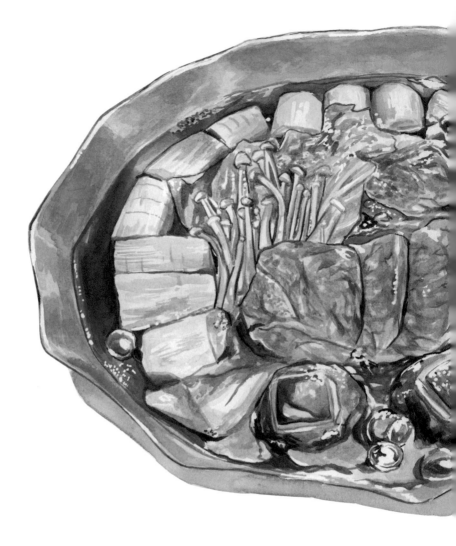

江戶時期（1603～1868年）的日本非常和平，
與國外沒有太多交流。
日本有很多傳統料理都是從江戶時代開始流傳下來的。
「江戶」一詞有時也會被當成等同「東京」的意義使用。

The Edo Period in Japan (1603-1868) was known for peace and prosperity
as well as for being a time with little foreign influence. The term "Edo" can also
refer to the Tokyo area. Many food traditions come from the Edo Period.

72 大蔥鮪魚火鍋
Negima Hotpot

一文名代 江戶大蔥鮪魚火鍋
淺草 酒膳一文 本店
2人份4400日圓

江戶時期鮪魚肚不太受歡迎，經常被當作廢料丟棄。因為脂肪過多無法久放，所以被當成貧窮庶民的食物。不能將整條鮪魚徹底吃完非常浪費，因此有人開發出「大蔥鮪魚火鍋」這道料理，用大蔥去除鮪魚的腥味，打造出人人喜愛的美味。現在鮪魚肚成了高級食材，所以這道菜也從貧窮庶民的飲食變成高級料理了。

Edo Negima hotpot
Asakusa Shuzen Ichimon Head Shop
¥4400 for 2 people

In the Edo Period, the fatty part of the tuna wasn't well liked and was often thrown away. It preserved poorly and was considered a low-class food. In order to use all parts of the tuna, the "Negima Hotpot" was invented as negi onion counteracted the "fishy" smell of the tuna soup. However fatty tuna is now a delicacy, so this hotpot has become a much more luxurious dish.

73 鰻魚飯
Eel Over Rice

鰻魚飯

鰻魚助 東南屋 淺草

3960日圓〜

鰻魚也是美國不太常見的食物。第一次吃的時候我有點抗拒，但是漂亮的白肉魚和甘甜的醬汁、炭火燒烤的香味讓我喜歡上這個味道。據說這道料理源自日本橋的餐廳，現在廣受全日本喜愛。如果是在鰻魚助這種充滿雅趣的老店享用，鰻魚飯的美味就更加倍了！

Unaju (Eel Over Rice)
Nyorosuke Tatsumiya Asakusa
From ¥3960

Eel is another ingredient not commonly eaten in the US. To be honest, I was a little unsettled the first time I tried it as it seemed quite an odd thing to eat. However the taste of the beautiful white fish grilled and then topped with a flavorful, sweet sauce made me fall in love. It's said to date back to a shop in Nihonbashi, Tokyo, but is now beloved throughout Japan. Eating unaju at an old shop like Nyorosuke makes the whole experience even more delicious.

74 天婦羅與蕎麥麵
Tempura and Soba

天婦羅是16世紀從葡萄牙傳來日本的食物，當時食用油很貴，所以天婦羅是非常昂貴的食物。江戶時代食用油的價格下降，天婦羅越來越受歡迎，日本的師傅們便想出各種變化料理。蕎麥麵也是在江戶時代開始受歡迎，天婦羅與蕎麥麵搭配成為經典，至今仍廣受大眾喜愛。

※插圖僅供參考。

Tempura was first introduced to Japan in the 16th century via the Portuguese, and it was originally an expensive dish due to the amount of oil used. However, during the Edo Period, oil became more affordable, and Japanese chefs started selling tempura in new ways. Soba noodles, another food that became popular during the Edo Period, started being served alongside tempura, and the combination is still very popular today.

※This image is used for illustrative purposes only.

居酒屋

我不喝酒，但是我覺得日本的
居酒屋文化相當有趣。
居酒屋的種類和數量繁多，
對工作繁忙的人來說也很友善，
是個交朋友的好地方。

Izakayas, or pubs, are an interesting
aspect of Japanese culture. While I don't
drink alcohol, I am always intrigued at
the number and variety of pubs across
Japan. They are great places for even busy
people to make new friends in a warm
environment.

IZAKAYA

75 日本酒與季節料理
Sake and Seasonal Dishes

季節套餐

神樂坂KADO

3500日圓〜

居酒屋有趣的地方，在於晚餐的單點料理多過套餐料理。喜歡的酒或飲料都可以自由搭配。既有一整年都吃得到的經典料理，也有每間店使用當季食材搭配的季節料理。神樂坂KADO可以在座位上享用季節套餐，也可以在無座位區享用單點料理。

Seasonal Course Dishes

Kagurazaka Kado

From ¥3500

One thing interesting about izakayas is that most menu items are not full meals. Instead, they are more like appetizers or snacks that you that you can pair with different alcohols or beverages. Besides their regular menu items, many izakayas will also make special dishes featuring seasonal ingredients. At Kagurazaka Kado, you can enjoy full course meals in their tatami rooms or individual dishes in their standing area.

MAR.
3月的推薦

——— at ———

神樂坂 KADO

Kagurazaka Kado

→ ⌒75⌒ 日本酒與單點料理
Sake and Seasonal Dishes

位於神樂坂小巷弄
非常有趣的居酒屋

我很喜歡神樂坂。這裡有很多咖啡店和傳統的商店，非常適合當日往返的小旅行。在小巷弄裡走一小段，就會發現「神樂坂KADO」這間有點罕見的居酒屋。居酒屋通常都會有吧檯座和一般座位，但這間店的一般座位是榻榻米座，而且會把料理放在漂亮的托盤上。懷舊的裝潢醞釀出美好的氣氛，是個年輕人也能放鬆享受的地方。

An Interesting Izakaya
on a Back Street in Kagurazaka

I enjoy the area of Kagurazaka quite a bit. With many traditional shops and cafes, it's a fun place for a day trip. Wandering the back streets, you can find Kagurazaka Kado, a hidden gem of an izakaya. While most izakayas have counter seating, this shop takes a different approach. You will be given a cushion to seat yourself on the tatami mat floors, and be served on individual traditional tray tables. The retro decor of the shop adds to the atmosphere, making the whole experience fun and unique, and even young people can enjoy the space.

75 SHOP INFO → P216

左上：位於玄關區的無座位席，很適合小
酌一杯。　上：能放鬆享受用餐時光的
座位，讓人感受到日本老屋的美好。

Upper Left：A dirt-floored standing bar.
It's a great location to casually stop by for
a drink. Above: Relaxed floor seating on
cushions. Enjoy the ambience of an old
Japanese house.

到神樂坂散步吧！
Let's go for a walk
in Kagurazaka!

便利商店

對日本人來說已經習以為常，不過生活周遭有這麼多
便利商店，我覺得日本真的是一個幸福的國家。
24小時都可以買到生活用品和食物，服務也很棒。
熱愛美食的我也非常喜歡日本便利商店的食物。

Japanese people don't realize how lucky they are to have such amazing
convenience stores. Open 24 hours and selling food and day-to-day
items, the quality and service is quite astounding.
As a food lover, I have no shame in revealing that I am a huge fan of
Japanese convenience store food.

76 便當
Bento

幕之內便當
7-11

美國的便利商店只有賣餅乾、飲
料、便宜的炸物和三明治。當然，
這些日本都有，除此之外日本便利
商店還有販售種類非常驚人的便
當。從日式到中式，甚至連西洋風
味的便當都有，而且還頻繁地推出
新產品，完全不會吃膩。

※目前可能已結束販售

''Wrapped-Up Favorites''
Bento
7-ELEVEN

US convenience stores usually carry
packaged snacks, beverages, cheap
fried foods, and sandwiches. These
are also available in Japan, but the
incredible number of bento lunch
boxes in Japanese convenience stores is
astounding. From traditional Japanese
flavors to Chinese and Western
varieties, they change out so frequently
that it's nearly impossible to get tired of
the selection.

※This item may not currently be for sale.

CONVENIENCE STORES

Bailene
Falls

蔬菜棒 附味噌美乃滋
7-11

我在便利商店最常購買的商品就是7-11
的「蔬菜棒 附味噌美乃滋」。雖然很簡
樸，但喜新厭舊的我從來不曾吃膩。來日
本之前，我只有在喝味噌湯的時候才會吃
到味噌，完全不知道味噌搭配美乃滋可以
變成最強醬汁！

Vegetable Sticks with Miso & Mayonnaise
7-ELEVEN

The convenience store food that I most repeatedly buy is the 7-Eleven Vegetable Sticks with Miso & Mayonnaise. While simple, it is the one item I have never tired of over the years. Before coming to Japan, I only knew miso as the soup, so this combination with mayo was a revelation!

77 SHOP INFO → P216

78 全家炸雞
Famichiki

全家炸雞

全家便利商店
180日圓

詢問回到母國的外國人:「你最想念的日本食物是什麼?」有好幾次對方都回答「全家炸雞」。便宜、單手就能拿起來吃,而且還非常美味,所以廣受日本人和外國人歡迎。

※此為2022年4月1日的價格

Famichiki

Family Mart
¥180

When friends leave Japan, I will sometimes ask them what things they will miss the most. In the food category, Family Mart's fried chicken "Famichiki" has been mentioned more than once. Cheap, portable, and insanely delicious, it's a favorite amongst both Japanese and foreigners alike.

※Current price as of April 1st, 2022.

SHOP INFO

59 築地青空三代目
築地青空三代目 / Tsukiji Aozora Sandaime

築地
Tsukiji

在高級的吧檯席上，以親民的價格享用嚴選食材的江戶前壽司。午餐時段的壽司可以選擇「午餐主廚精選」3520日圓～7150日圓。

📞 03-3541-1055
📍 東京都中央区築地4-13-8 トラスト築地KNビル1F
🚶 距離地鐵築地站本願寺出口徒步5分鐘

You can enjoy reasonably-priced, special Edo-Mae sushi at counter seating in this restaurant that feels very high-end. Their lunch menu "Lunch Omakase" runs from ¥3520 to ¥7150.

📞 +81 3-3541-1055
📍 Trust Tsukiji KN Building 1F
4-13-8 Tsukiji, Chuo-ku, Tokyo
🚶 5-min. walk from the Honganji Exit of the Tsukiji Subway Station

---

60 魚米 澀谷道玄坂店
魚べい 渋谷道玄坂店 / Uobei Shibuya Dogenzaka Store

澀谷
Shibuya

追求美味、趣味、速度，超越迴轉壽司的壽司餐廳。以110日圓料理為主，從老到小都能輕鬆享受美食。

📞 03-3462-0241
📍 東京都渋谷区道玄坂2-29-11 第6セントラルビル1F
🚶 距離各線澀谷站徒步約5分鐘

A sushi restaurant that goes above and beyond conveyor belt sushi, striving for deliciousness, fun, and speed. A majority of their sushi is priced at ¥110 and can be enjoyed by young and old alike.

📞 +81 3-3462-0241
📍 6th Central Building 1F
2-29-11 Dogenzaka, Shibuya-ku, Tokyo
🚶 5-min. walk from Shibuya Station

61 銀座帆掛

銀座ほかけ / Ginza Hokake

昭和12年開業的壽司老店。食材本身品質就非常優良，可以充分享受江戶前壽司以醃漬或燉煮等手法為基礎的妙趣。

📞 03-6383-3300
📍 東京都中央区銀座4-10-6 銀料ビル1F
🚇 距離地鐵銀座站徒步約2分鐘

A long-established sushi restaurant founded in 1945. Enjoy Edo-Mae sushi which emphasizes not only the quality of the ingredients but also classic preparations including seasoning and boiling.

📞 +81 3-6383-3300
📍 Ginryo Building 1F
4-10-6 Ginza, Chuo-ku, Tokyo
🚇 2-min. walk from the Higashi-Ginza Subway Station

62 福壽家

福寿家 / Fukujuya

大正11年開業的老店。高級稻荷壽司專賣店。嚴選豆皮、白米、自製滷汁，獨創前所未有的稻荷壽司。

📞 03-5828-3787
📍 東京都台東区花川戸2-18-6
🚇 距離地鐵淺草站徒步約6分鐘

A shop with a long history, founded in 1922 and specializing in high-quality inari sushi. This store also serves new and original varieties of inari sushi, taking great pride in their fried tofu skins, rice, and homemade broth.

📞 +81 3-5828-3787
📍 2-18-6 Hanakawado, Taito-Ku, Tokyo
🚇 6-min. walk from the Asakusa Subway Station

63 數字牛奶糖 表參道店

ナンバーシュガー 表参道店 /
NUMBER SUGAR Omotesando Shop

表参道
Omotesando

使用無添加、無染色、無防腐劑的天然食材。販售古法製作的經典牛奶糖與各種口味的牛奶糖。

📞 03-6427-3334
📍 東京都渋谷区神宮前 5-11-11 1F
🚃 距離地鐵表參道站A1號出口徒步5分鐘

A candy shop that uses natural additive-free, artificial-color-free, and preservative-free ingredients. They sell classic caramels in a variety of flavors, all made the old-fashioned way.

📞 +81 3-6427-3334
📍 1F 5-11-11 Jingumae, Shibuya-ku, Tokyo
🚃 5-min. walk from the A1 Exit of the Omotesando Subway Station

64 銀座 綠壽庵清水

銀座 緑寿庵清水 / Ginza Ryokujuan Shimizu

銀座
Ginza

全日本僅此一間的金平糖專賣店。金平糖的製造工法相當困難，綠壽庵清水以獨傳一子的形式傳承至今，打造出只有銀座 綠壽庵清水才能呈現的好味道。

📞 03-5537-9111
📍 東京都中央区銀座 6-2-1 Daiwa 銀座ビル1F
🚃 距離地鐵銀座站C2出口徒步5分鐘

The only konpeito specialty shop in Japan. Konpeito is very difficult to produce, and the ones produced at Ginza Ryokujuan Shimizu are like no other. The techniques are passed down from generation to generation, only one person at a time.

📞 +81 3-5537-9111
📍 Daiwa Ginza Building 1F
6-2-1 Ginza, Chuo-ku, Tokyo
🚃 5-min. walk from the C2 Exit of the Ginza Subway Station

65 harapecolab

ハラペコラボ / harapecolab

福岡縣
Fukuoka Prefecture

從和菓子琥珀糖發想製作，以礦物為設計藍本的「礦物和菓子」。讓人可以同時享受宛如真正寶石般的外觀與口感。

📞 092-710-1136
📍 福岡県福岡市南区大池1-26-7義道ハイム1F
🚃 距離西鐵天神大牟田線高宮站車程約7分鐘

This shop sells "Koubutsu Wokashi" sweets made from amber sugar to look like crystals. You can enjoy both the interesting texture and jeweled appearance of these Japanese sweets.

📞 +81 92-710-1136
📍 Yoshimichi Heim 1F
   1-26-7 Oike, Minami-ku, Fukuoka-shi, Fukuoka
🚃 7 minutes by car from Takamiya Station on the Nishitetsu Tenjin-Omuta Line

66 INITIAL 中目黑

イニシャル中目黒 / INITIAL Nakameguro

中目黒
Nakameguro

以甜點搭配酒類為主題，成熟大人專屬的漂亮聖代廣受矚目。在各種時間點提供能夠畫下完美「句點」的華麗聖代。

📞 03-6452-4994
📍 東京都目黒区上目黒1-16-6 ナチュラルスクエアビル 1F
🚃 距離東急東横線中目黒站徒步約2分鐘

Beautiful "grown-up" parfaits made with the concept of a marrying dessert and liquor. Providing gorgeous desserts that excite the tastebuds differently at various stages of eating.

📞 +81 3-6452-4994
📍 Natural Square Building 1F
   1-16-6 Kamimeguro, Meguro-ku, Tokyo
🚃 5-min. walk from the Nakameguro Station on the Tokyu Toyoko line

67 法國英鎊屋

フレンチパウンドハウス / FRENCH POUND HOUSE

知名的草莓奶油蛋糕，使用大量草莓與優質鮮奶油，以及稍微浸泡草莓果汁的海綿蛋糕製作，堪稱奶油蛋糕界的逸品。店內空間以藍色為基調，整體非常優雅。

📞 03-3944-2108
📍 東京都豊島区巣鴨1-4-4 マンション サンビップ巣鴨1F
🚶 距離JR巣鴨站徒步約5分鐘

Their famous strawberry shortcake consists of strawberries, high-quality cream, and sponge cake soaked lightly in strawberry juice. The store's beautiful blue-color provides an elegant environment in which to enjoy your dessert.

📞 +81 3-3944-2108
📍 Mansion Sunvip Sugamo 1F
　 1-4-4 Sugamo, Toshima-ku, Tokyo
🚶 5-min. walk from the JR Sugamo Station

70 虎屋 赤坂店

とらや 赤坂店 / Toraya Akasaka Shop

擁有將近500年歷史的和菓子店。最具代表性的商品是煉羊羹，從煮紅豆到完工需要耗費3天的時間。每一樣甜點都是用心製作，都很適合當作伴手禮。

📞 03-3408-2331
📍 東京都港区赤坂4-9-22
🚶 距離地鐵赤坂見附站徒步約7分鐘

A Japanese confectionery store with roughly 500 years of history. Their classic yokan takes 3 days from boiling azuki beans to completion. All their carefully crafted sweets make perfect souvenirs.

📞 +81 3-3408-2331
📍 4-9-22 Akasaka, Minato-ku, Tokyo
🚶 7-min. walk from the Akasaka-Mitsuke Subway Station

72 淺草 酒膳一文 本店

淺草 酒膳一文 本店 / Asakusa Shuzen Ichimon Head Shop

這是一間在屋齡65年的獨棟建築內，保留舊式泥土地面，充滿情調的大江戶居酒屋。我推薦名代江戶大蔥鮪魚火鍋、名代料理一文燒賣、合鴨雞絞肉。

📞 03-3875-6800
📍 東京都台東区浅草3-12-6
🚃 距離筑波快線淺草站徒步約3分鐘

This Oedo izakaya pub is located in a 65-year-old building with dirt floors that lend to the historic atmosphere. Their "Edo Negima" Nabe comes highly recommended alongside their famous steamed dumplings and duck meatballs.

📞 +81 3-3875-6800
📍 3-12-6 Asakusa, Taito-ku, Tokyo
🚃 5-min. walk from the Asakusa Station on the Tsukuba Express Line

73 鰻魚助 東南屋 淺草

にょろ助 東南屋 淺草 / Nyorosuke Tatsumiya Asakusa

距離淺草寺的仲見世通徒步約1分鐘。使用自江戶時代以來，在下町地區就廣受喜愛的鰻魚和泥鰍等食材，製作傳統日本料理。

📞 03-3842-7373
📍 東京都台東区浅草1-33-5
🚃 距離地鐵淺草站徒步約1分鐘

A one-minute walk from Nakamise Street by Sensoji Temple. You can enjoy traditional Japanese cuisine using eels and loaches that have been enjoyed in the area since the Edo period.

📞 +81 3-3842-7373
📍 1-33-5 Asakusa, Taito-ku, Tokyo
🚃 1-min. walk from the Asakusa Subway Station

75 **神樂坂 KADO**
神樂坂カド / Kagurazaka Kado

將老宅直接當作店面，充滿懷舊氛圍的居酒屋。
有一般座位，也有可以站著小酌一杯的無座位
席。到神樂坂散步的時候，務必順便繞過去。

℡ 03-3268-2410
⌖ 東京都新宿区赤城元町1-32
🏠 距離地鐵神樂坂站徒步約3分鐘

An izakaya with a nostalgic atmosphere located in an
old private house. You can stand and drink in the dirt
floor room or sit and drink in the tatami room. Swing
by after taking a walk in the Kagurazaka area.

℡ +81 3-3268-2410
⌖ 1-32 Akagi-Motomachi, Shinjuku-ku, Tokyo
🏠 3-min. walk from the Kagurazaka Subway
Station

76·77 **7-11**
7-ELEVEN

以「又近又方便」為宗旨的便利商店。提供多元
豐富的商品和服務，以生活基礎建設為目標，持
續進行各種不同的挑戰。

℡ 03-6238-3711（總公司）
⌖ 東京都內約有2800間分店，日本國內約有2萬
1330間分店（2022年3月底）

A convenience store with the motto "close and
convenient." With a large number of products
and services, they continue to evolve to meet the
challenges and the lifestyle needs of the community.

℡ +81 3-6238-3711
⌖ About 2,800 stores in Tokyo／21,330 stores
in Japan

PART 2

描繪寫實
水彩插畫的祕訣

Tips for Creating Realistic
Watercolor Paintings.

水彩畫有很多技巧，這裡介紹的是描繪寫實
風格的食物時，我會注意的重點。

While there are many different techniques for
watercolor painting, here are some of my tips for
making realistic food illustrations.

1 水彩畫無法清除畫過的痕跡，所以在開
始上色前，決定好需要呈現光澤的純白
反光點一定要用「遮蓋液」保護。

2 請不要把顏色想得很簡單。紅色不只是
紅色，而是確實分析是帶紫的紅還是偏
橘的紅，然後再進行混色。

3 請分成多層上色。按照顏色淡到深的順
序上色，利用水彩的透明度，才能呈現
複雜又漂亮的顏色。

4 最後再加上細節以及「輪廓線」。每次
用水的時候顏色都會暈開，所以在途中
加入細節沒有意義。因此，最後再加上
細節吧！

1 Watercolor can't be erased, so before you
begin painting, find all your highlights
and use masking fluid to protect them.

2 Stop thinking of colors in a simple
manner. For example, rather than just
"red," decide if it's a purple red or an
orange red. Try to carefully analyze each
color before painting it.

3 Use a lot of layers. Start with light colors
and gradually build to darker colors. This
way, you can use the transparency
of watercolor to create a piece with
beautiful and complicated colors.

4 Save the details and hard edges until
the end. As you use water, the edges
will soften, so adding details too early
is a waste of time. Wait to add details
until the very end to bring everything
together.

BEHIND THE SCENES

i made a friend!

下次要畫什麼呢～

我要開動了！

out for a stroll ♬

SHOP INDEX

SHOP INDEX

日本百味散步帳：四季都好吃的一期一繪 /KAILENE FALLS 著 . -- 初版 . -- 臺北市：時報文化出版企業股份有限公司 , 2023.11

224 面 ; 14.8*21 公分

ISBN 978-626-374-424-0(平裝)

1.CST: 遊記 2.CST: 飲食風俗 3.CST: 水彩畫 4.CST: 日本

731.9   112016210

ISBN 978-626-374-424-0

Printed in Taiwan

ACROSS074

日本百味散步帳

四季都好吃的一期一繪

作者 凱琳・芙爾斯（KAILENE FALLS）｜**翻譯** 涂紋凰｜**主編** 尹蘊雯｜**責任編輯** 王瓊苹｜**責任企劃** 吳美瑤｜**封面設計** 張巖｜**內頁排版** 洪伊珊｜**副總編** 邱憶伶｜**董事長** 趙政岷｜**出版者**｜時報文化出版企業股份有限公司｜108019 臺北市和平西路 3 段 240 號 3 樓｜**發行專線**（02)23066842｜**讀者服務專線**（0800)231705・(02)23047103｜**讀者服務傳真**（02)23046858｜**郵撥** 19344724 時報文化出版公司｜**信箱** 10899 臺北華江橋郵局第 99 信箱｜**時報悅讀網** http://www.readingtimes.com.tw｜**電子郵件信箱** newlife@readingtimes.com.tw｜**時報出版愛讀者** http://www.facebook.com/readingtimes.2｜**法律顧問** 理律法律事務所 陳長文律師、李念祖律師｜**印刷**｜華展印刷有限公司｜**初版一刷** 2023 年 11 月 10 日｜**定價** 新臺幣 480 元